SPAIN:

AN INTERPRETATION

AMS PRESS

NEW YORK

ANGEL GANIVET
1865-1898

SPAIN:

AN INTERPRETATION

With Introduction by
R. M. Nadal

1946
LONDON:
EYRE & SPOTTISWOODE

Library of Congress Cataloging in Publication Data

Ganivet, Angel, 1865-1898.
  Spain.

  Translation of Idearium español.
  Reprint of the 1946 ed. published by Eyre &
Spottiswoode, London.
  1. National characteristics, Spanish. I. Title.
DP52.G2713   1976   946   75-41109
ISBN 0-404-14755-0

Reprinted from the edition of 1946, London
First AMS edition published in 1976
Manufactured in the United States of America

AMS PRESS INC.
NEW YORK, N. Y.

CONTENTS

INTRODUCTION 9

A

PSYCHOLOGICAL CONSTITUTION OF THE SPANISH SOUL. VIRGIN SPAIN
AND "SENEQUISMO"; CHRISTIANITY AND CATHOLICISM; THE TERRI-
TORIAL SPIRIT; SPANISH SPIRIT OF INDEPENDENCE AS SEEN: (a) IN
HER ARMY, (b) IN HER LAW, (c) IN HER ART.

Pages 25 to 76

B

SPAIN'S FOREIGN POLICY. INTERPRETATION OF SPANISH HISTORY;
RELATIONS WITH ENGLAND—GIBRALTAR; PORTUGAL AND PENINSU-
LAR UNITY; IBEROAMÉRICA; THE MEDITERRANEAN; SPAIN'S
COLONIAL SYSTEM; MOROCCO.

Pages 77 to 115

C

DIAGNOSIS OF PRESENT EVILS AND THEIR REMEDY. TASK OF SPAIN;
THE SPANISH DISEASE: ABOULIA; THE REMEDY: RESTORATION OF THE
SPIRITUAL LIFE OF SPAIN.

Pages 117 to 136

TRANSLATOR'S NOTE

IN the vast literature of Spain no small space is occupied by a series of works to whose writers has been given the name of *arbitristas*. They have discussed the problems, special or general, with which at different periods their country has been faced, and have proposed their own particular solutions. Ganivet's book stands out from the ruck by the fact that it is an attempt to formulate a philosophy of Spanish history, and to deduce therefrom the direction which he hoped Spain would follow in the future. As the date on the title-page shows, nearly half a century has passed since the author's death, which occurred in the very year which saw the destruction of the remnants of what was once the mighty Spanish Empire. The tragedy of Spain and the tragedy of Ganivet thus went hand-in-hand. The span of threescore years and ten which mortals have been encouraged to hope for would have allowed him to live till near the present day, and the reader of this his best-known book can hardly fail to ask himself what Ganivet would have thought of all that has happened to Spain since the year 1898.

Only the bare facts of Angel Ganivet's life will be noted here. Born in Granada in 1865 of working-class stock, he had little education in early years owing to the premature death of his father. When later it was undertaken by the help of friends, the boy showed distinct promise, and after the usual secondary-school course entered the university of his native town and graduated in the Faculty of Philosophy and Letters. At the age of 24 he was appointed to a post in a section of the Records Office in Madrid and, continuing his studies, obtained his Doctorate at the Central University. In 1892 he entered the Consular Service and was appointed

Vice-Consul at Antwerp. This post was followed by that of Consul in Helsingfors (Finland) and in Riga when the consulate was transferred there in 1898. A few months after taking up his duties in the latter place he perished by his own act in the waters of the Dwina. Much has been written about the intimate tragedy of his existence, thus untimely closed. This is not the place to draw aside the charitable veil provided by the official death certificate issued by the Russian authorities: "died by drowning, while of unsound mind", and by the medical diagnosis made a short time previously: "progressive paralysis and persecution mania".

In addition to the book here translated, the bibliography of Ganivet includes two novels, descriptive writings on his native Granada, a selection of correspondence and a poetical drama. No analysis of content or form of the present work will be attempted here, but its place in modern Spanish thought may be indicated. Along with Unamuno's slightly earlier essays, *En Torno al Casticismo*, it formed the advance guard of the legion of books that have since been produced on the burning question of the "regeneration" of Spain. Practically all writers on the subject have acknowledged the influence of Ganivet's book, which is continually re-issued in Spain, and fresh interest was recently given to it on the occasion of the transference of the mortal remains of the author to his native soil. It is a proof at once of the breadth of view and of the strain of inconsistency which has been noted in the book, that parties widely differing in ideals rivalled in doing honour to his memory and claiming him as their own. The Introduction written for this English version by a Spaniard of the present generation will serve to indicate that Ganivet's book still exerts its influence.

It may be added that the translation now published was made as far back as 1925, and appears by arrangement with the author's son, Don Angel Ganivet Roldán. A very few notes, which seemed necessary, have been placed at the end.

INTRODUCTION

*S*PAIN: *An Interpretation.* This is the well-chosen title
given by the translator to the English version of Angel
Ganivet's *Idearium Español*, for that is exactly what is
contained in these pages of "free flowing meditation", as
Unamuno called them. Why, it may be asked, choose this
particular interpretation and not that of Unamuno himself,
or of Costa, or of Ortega y Gasset? Simply because, in spite
of evident defects due to the idiosyncrasies of the author, it
is here that we find the deepest understanding of the Spanish
soul; because, though some of the observations are out of
date and some of the judgments erroneous, the problem
stated by Ganivet is the same that preóccupies Spaniards
to-day; and because no other book has had so much influence
—whether by acceptance or rejection—on contemporary
Spanish thought and on foreign students of Spain. The first
reason justifies the two following, and all combined give this
book a renewed actuality now that Spain is passing through
another critical period of her history.

In his examination of the idealistic basis of Spain, Ganivet
proceeds from essence to form; from the spirit to its manifestation; from peninsular Spain to the higher cultural unity
of the Spanish-speaking world. He studies Spain's position
in regard to Europe, and the considerations which should
determine her attitude to other countries; in particular,
Great Britain and Portugal. His frank discussion of the
problems of his time, his examination of possible solutions of
international questions, give us the impression that we are
reading the notes of an observer of our own day.

What is the underlying thought of this book, and what
criticism of it can be offered?

Attracted by the phenomenon of the rise and fall of the

9

Spanish Empire, historians have discussed at length the causes thereof. With eyes steadily fixed on the main outlines, they tend to overlook the final period of that long-drawn-out crisis, the tragic ninety years which constitute Spain's nineteenth century: 1808-1898.

.In the eighteenth century, Spain still bestirs herself to fall into line with the general course of European life. This in spite of the fact that her international prestige was continuing on the downward curve started in the previous century. Notwithstanding heavy foreign commitments, important and necessary reforms in home affairs were taken in hand. The dominant ideas are those prevailing in the rest of Europe; in the attempted solution of the many problems we discover a continental technique adapted to the circumstances of Spain. The same cannot be said of the nineteenth century. Spain—for good as well as for ill—has had no nineteenth century in the strictly European sense. What characterises Spain to-day is the fact that current ideas and problems are pressing upon a people who have not yet found a solution to the ideological struggles and material problems of the last century.

In stressing the failure of the Spanish nineteenth century, there is no necessary implication of national defects or collective incapacity. Spain had to deal with a combination of unfortunate events, many entirely unavoidable, falling upon an organism worn out by an excess of foreign activities in previous centuries. One should remember some of those events, because they are the determining factors in the trend of Spanish thought at the end of the nineteenth century.

They may be presented in tabular form:

The Napoleonic Invasion and the War of Independence (1808-1814).

The Intervention of the Holy Alliance (1823).

Two long and bloody civil wars (1833-1839 and 1872-1876).

Six written constitutions and others which remained in embryo.

The long series of *pronunciamientos*, by which the army takes a hand in political strife, begins in 1823.

It is against this peninsular background that one has to project the struggle for independence of the American Provinces. The close of the century brings the war with the United States (1898), in which Spain lost the remnants of her overseas empire.

These calamities occur during the time when Europe is carrying out the great Industrial Revolution, when new nations and new empires are springing up. If in addition we recall that these misfortunes fall upon a people who, since the beginning of the Reconquest in the eighth century, had enjoyed hardly a moment's respite, we shall marvel that Spain survived as a nation; that there was still left energy sufficient to build from the ruins a new Spain. But the Spaniards of the nineteenth century could only perceive that they were overcoming one difficulty to face a greater, that the external splendour of past centuries had been changed into internal poverty and ruin, although what was still left was a people full of physical and moral reserves. Is it surprising then that in the closing years of the century a theme whose first manifestations are to be found in some writers of the Golden Age should take on the character of an obsession? For an obsession, and rightly so, is this constant reinterpretation of the Spanish phenomenon, this searching for causes and explanations of failures, this laying down of lines for a national revival. This preoccupation runs through all the writings of the choicest spirits at the end of the century, when Spain, after various centuries of discovery, colonisation and world empire, finds herself alone, enclosed within the strict geographical limits of the home country. Such is the collective state of mind which produces, amongst other books, the essay by Ganivet to which he gave the title of *Idearium Español*.

Symbolically, Ganivet uses the first three letters of the alphabet as headings for the sections into which the work is divided:—

A—Psychological constitution of the Spanish soul.
B—Spain's foreign policy.
C—Diagnosis of present evils and their remedy.

Ganivet holds that the ultimate element in the idealistic foundation of Spain is stoicism—"the natural, human stoicism of Seneca", the Spanish philosopher *par excellence*. Its later contact with Christianity may be likened to the meeting of two travellers from opposite directions, "each of whom will have to cover the road previously traversed by the other". This Christian stoicism is later brought face to face with Islam, and from the resulting clash there spring the most marked tendencies in the religious spirit of Spain— mysticism (which is for Ganivet "the sanctification of African sensuality") and fanaticism (meaning for him "the turning against ourselves when the Reconquest was completed, of the fury accumulated during eight centuries of combat").

It is true that Ganivet was not the first to speak of the secret of this stoic cast in the Spanish character. The references to Seneca and his influence go far back in the literature of Spain, but, as has been observed, "if Ganivet did not make the discovery, he gave form to the idea and put it into wide circulation". Doubtless this primitive stoicism—if it did exist—underwent transformations with the development of Christianity in Spain. Still clearer is the supposition that eight centuries of life in contact with Islam produced, for good and evil, as many deflections in the national spirit as it did in the history. In the course of centuries the sharp effects have been much blunted, but this combination of stoicism, mysticism and fanaticism still shows itself, and not only in the field of religious beliefs.

In his analysis of the psychological structure of Spain, Ganivet is not satisfied with discovering what he very confusedly calls "the external mechanism". He thinks that religion—for all its deep roots—is not the deepest element in a nation, "for religion changes". Something more permanent must be looked for, "the nucleus round which cling all the folds that in the course of time transform the physiognomy of a country". As the one thing permanent with us is the land, this nucleus is to be found in the "territorial spirit".

Here we have the framework on which the author is going to build up a great part of his theory. It is a commonplace that the geographical factor enters into the manner of life

and even the psychology of the inhabitants of different
regions. But Ganivet carries this admitted influence to
extreme lengths. He finds a specific characteristic for the
inhabitants of continents, peninsulas and islands—the
respective labels being "resistance", "independence" and
"aggression"; though he recognises for all of them the same
governing principle: "self-preservation". As examples of the
three groups he cites France, Spain and England, and
attempts to find support for his theory in the history of the
three countries. Much of what he says is ingenious and to
the point, but the principle cannot be accepted as absolute.
Ganivet passes over in silence the history of other continental
countries, other islands and peninsulas which would
contradict the theory as formulated. And here we notice
some of his radical defects: arbitrary generalisation, an
attitude of paradox, a certain wildness of statement, and
from time to time a not always graceful Andalusian pirouette.
But alongside these defects what skilled observation, what
restrained passion, how much essential truth! He sees the
spirit of independence as distinctive of the peninsula, the
spirit of individualism as characteristic of its inhabitants,
and when describing how these traits manifest themselves
in the military, the juridical and the artistic spheres, the
author discovers for us the innermost recesses of the soul of
Spain.

If the characteristic of the peninsula is the spirit of
independence and not of aggression, how are we to understand the modern history of Spain, in which from the
moment of its formation she stands out as a warlike and
conquering nation? Ganivet's interpretation is that the
spirit of aggression has indeed existed, but only as a "transformation" of the spirit of independence, and that it will
gradually disappear with the disappearance of the causes
which produced that transformation. The metamorphosis
is explained by a fact which at first sight seems to lack
explanation: the prolonged duration of Moorish domination
in Spain. "The completion of the Reconquest is ardently
desired, but there is fear about what will come after. The
triumph of Christianity is the object in view, but there is
another important matter, not to be overlooked—the

preservation of the independence of the different portions of territory and their charter privileges."

"The first result of the Reconquest", says the great Spanish medievalist, Sánchez-Albornoz, "was the bursting into new life of Iberian individualism", beaten down after a long struggle by the Romans and the Goths. The jealousies and rivalries of the various Christian kingdoms explain this slowness of the Reconquest, the opposing lines of expansion followed, the lack of co-ordination of effort. Whilst recognising its insufficiency, we may find some reason for Ganivet's affirmation that while other countries start on a career of conquest through excess of strength, Spain, lacking strength, conquers in order to acquire it.

Fourteen-ninety-two is a year decisive in the history of Spain. The Reconquest is over, peninsular unity almost completed and Spain finds herself at the crossroads. She goes forward in all directions with incredible vigour, maintaining her European hegemony during the greater part of the sixteenth century. But it was at the cost of forgetting what should have been her primary duty—the establishment of "true and intimate national unity", the links of which were still very weak. Yet the decision taken was not entirely a voluntary one. "The Castilian policy", writes Ganivet, "was a southern one—Africa; the Aragonese, an eastern one—the Mediterranean." A good case could be made out for both. Again: "The discoveries and conquests of America . . . had their justification in our character, in our faith, and in the providential destiny which laid such a heavy burden on our shoulders. But our action in the centre of the Continent was an immeasurable political absurdity." This is a judgment which from different viewpoints and with different arguments has been accepted by practically all historians.

If in the past Spain scattered her energies over the four points of the compass, Ganivet urges the need for laying down clearly what are the actual external interests of Spain, so that her internal organisation may be based on them. He begins with the north. "Our former fatal continental policy is outworn, dead and buried." It has become fashionable of late to talk of the "good-neighbour policy". In the history of the last hundred years it would be difficult to find a country which has gone further than Spain in regulating its external policy in accordance with this sound principle. Spain is of course helped in this by the natural alignment of her frontiers and by the lesson of past mistakes. But more than anything, she is moved by the conviction deeply rooted in the national conscience that any intervention in purely European matters lies outside the country's natural sphere of action. Spain maintained her neutrality during the war of 1914-1918, and in spite of all prophecies she remained neutral in the recent struggle. On both occasions there was a variety of causes, but the determining factor has been this keen national conscience. Voluntary semi-isolation by no means implies indifference to the fate of Europe. Apart from the fact that Spain's universalist spirit renders such a notion impossible, she knows by long experience that she can never be unconcerned by the fate of a continent of which she is quite definitely a part. Her interest is derived therefore not only from a sense of universal justice, but also from the knowledge of the repercussions which international strife may have on her own internal life. With this in mind, the position of Spain in regard to Europe is so clear to Ganivet that the two countries to which he gives special attention both lie outside the Continent proper: Great Britain and Portugal.

One might say that for Ganivet, Spain, as an Atlantic-Mediterranean peninsula, is linked with Great Britain on all sides except on the one which separates her from the Continent—the Pyrenean frontier. Ganivet has hard words to say of England, but this does not prevent him from facing realities and estimating their influence on the future. "Among all European nations", he writes, "Spain is, after Italy, the one most interested in the preservation, for as long as possible, of England's naval supremacy." Two reasons are given to support this statement. The first is one which Sancho Panza would approve: "Better the devil you know than the devil you don't know." Before childishly rejoicing at the downfall of England, one should think which power will take her place. "We ourselves cannot be England's heirs; and we must ask ourselves who is to be the inheritor in the event of her overthrow." The second—a more profound reason—is clear to everyone to-day, but in 1896 had something prophetic in it: "England has reached the zenith of her powers of absorption and she is now obliged to resort to a defensive procedure." The nation which possesses an empire ceases to be imperialistic. Danger only arises from those who have never had one. At the close of the last century Ganivet seemed to fear that the sudden disappearance of the British Empire would constitute one of those cataclysms whose effects extend to all countries and most of all to the weakest. Consequently, the existence and gradual evolution of the British Empire is something affecting others besides the empire's component parts, provided always that in the prosecution of "defensive methods" reciprocal interests with other countries are kept in view. None other is the meaning of Ganivet when he says that "the power of Great Britain would be useful to Europe if, deprived of her aggressiveness, she continued to exist as an agent of public international order".

Nevertheless, that nation to which Spain is attached by so many and by such varied interests is precisely the one against which Spain has a real motive for resentment— Gibraltar. Ganivet puts the problem in its right setting. "The ransom of Gibraltar must be a task essentially and exclusively Spanish." "Gibraltar is a permanent offence . . . but it does not hinder the normal development of the nation nor is it a sufficient cause for us to sacrifice more valuable interests in order to anticipate an event the realisation of which will be a logical result of the restoration of our nationality." The question of Gibraltar should, therefore, never be a motive for Spain's entering a coalition against England, the result of which might well be its substitution by a more dangerous power.

Here we have Ganivet once again voicing a national sentiment which has since undergone no change, as was proved in the critical months between 1940 and 1943. It is true that bands of youths, incited by German agents, occasionally threw stones at the British Embassy and went through the streets of the capital demanding the return of

Gibraltar. Nevertheless, the lack of popular enthusiasm behind those manifestations does not imply a lack of interest in the fate of Gibraltar. The truth is that within the limits stated by Ganivet it is a problem felt to-day as yesterday by Spaniards of all parties, not excluding the friends of Great Britain in Spain. Gibraltar, in fact, appears to the majority of Spaniards as a *terra irredenta*. But it is difficult for them to see the possibility, even the advantage, of its immediate liberation. Stern facts are here opposed to theory and sentiment. It is realised that as long as the Mediterranean continues to be a vital means of communication and sea warfare remains decisive, and as long as Great Britain has interests in the Near and Far East, she will not abandon Gibraltar, and it is possibly to the interest of Spain that England should have, while these conditions prevail, obligations in the Straits. It is irrelevant that the strategic importance of the Rock is to-day practically neutralised; nor will many Spaniards think this constitutes a reason to accept changes. Neverthless, a condominium, or some other legal formula combining the efficiency of the *status quo* with the recognition of the natural rights of Spain, would contribute towards the disappearance of the only motive for resentment which, though silent, is keenly felt.

Turning to Portugal our author is grieved to see the map of the peninsula "printed in two different colours". He mourns the incomplete peninsular unity, but, unlike the majority of his countrymen, he does not attribute the actual state of affairs to the work of "perfidious Albion", but to lack of will on the part of the two countries concerned. Ideal as such a union would be, in order to avoid the natural suspicion of Portugal it could only be attained if and when Portugal desired. In the meantime, Ganivet thinks that "it is better to live apart and treat each other like brothers than to live together amid constant bickerings".

This part of the *Idearium* is animated by a profound realistic sense. Ganivet stresses Spain's interest in the whole Mediterranean policy, though the reasons he advances have by now lost their actuality. As Spain has not sufficient strength to make her voice heard, he declares himself in favour of the Mediterranean *status quo*. The logical policy of Spanish expansion, once the Reconquest was ended, could and should have been penetration towards the south. To initiate such a policy to-day would be stark madness. But an abstentionist policy is not possible in Morocco. "Spain has an interest, too clear to require proof, in keeping territory on the opposite side of the Straits as far removed as possible from European political action." Unfortunately, the Treaty of Algeciras (1906), which Ganivet did not live to see, left the problem open and no solution satisfactory to Spain has yet been found.

The salvation of Spain cannot come from any foreign country, nor can it be sought in any activity outside the peninsula. External interests can only be defended from inside. None of them suggests or requires a dispersal of energy abroad. These are the conclusions arrived at by Ganivet in his examination of Spain's foreign policy. They are the same principles to which Spain has tacitly adhered for many years with a continuity which is in startling contrast with the many vicissitudes of her home policy. For Ganivet the salvation of Spain can be worked out only within Spain herself, in the concentration of all her energies inside her own territory. He concludes this section of his essay with what he calls an adaptation from St. Augustine: "*Noli foras ire, in interiore Hispaniae habitat veritas.*"

How did Ganivet see this interior of Spain?

"Spain lives in perpetual civil war." So wrote Ganivet in 1896, and this phrase alone would justify the actuality still enjoyed by his book. He believes he can trace the cause. "The Spanish temperament, excited and weakened by endless periods of strife, seems powerless to undergo a transformation. Hence all those who become enthusiastic for an idea change it into a weapon of strife." This transformation is not an easy one; it has no precedent in history. "Spain was the first European nation to be aggrandised by a policy of expansion and conquest; it was the first to decline, and it is the first which has now to work towards a political and social restoration of a new order."

What is the nature of this transformation so repeatedly referred to by Ganivet? Nothing less than a leap from the material to the spiritual. With all her energies dedicated to internal reconstruction once her house is set in order, Spain, "by an effort of her intelligence, might reconstruct the family circle of all Hispanic peoples". It is not a question of an impossible reconstruction of her past empire, nor of artificial political or commercial unions, but of the establishment of a culture based on similarity of ideals. Ganivet wrote in the same century in which Spain lost her American provinces, but already he was able to see all Spanish-speaking peoples forming a unity of culture. Being the first to notice the phenomenon he is in a sense the precursor of the concept of "Hispanidad", which has been so badly misinterpreted and misused by the Falange in recent years.

In the Spain of the end of the century Ganivet, however, could perceive neither the intelligence required to understand this enterprise nor the will to engage in it. He diagnosed the infirmity which afflicted Spaniards as collective *aboulia*. The lack of a synthetic sense which such an infirmity involves and the excitability caused by prolonged external activity produce a condition whose main feature is the sterile recollection of past achievements. If a new idea is acquired "as it lacks any counterweight, there is a passage from atony to exaltation; the 'fixed idea' leads to 'violent impulse' ". The symptoms are accurately described, but did the infirmity really exist? During the turbulent history of the nineteenth century, whenever there is an interval of relative normality, a glimpse of wise direction from above with a minimum of liberty, the Spanish people respond admirably. On the ruins of the country, a great statesman, Cánovas del Castillo—by methods which would be inadmissible to-day, but which corresponded to the realities and the needs of his time—built up the framework of a modern state. At once there was a vigorous revival in the political, economic and social life of the whole country. Ganivet made his diagnosis of *aboulia* at the very time when important reforms were being planned or were beginning to be carried out. He criticised the universities at a moment when inside and outside official circles new centres of educational research were being created to prepare for the cultural and scientific developments of the Spain of to-day. And when Ganivet thought that Spain was "inattentive in the midst of the world" new social doctrines were appearing in the country and taking root there; labour parties and trade unions were making their appearance on the political stage. But, we must repeat, Ganivet was writing under the direct influence of his own century. Like the rest of his contemporaries he did not fully realise the burden laid by that century on the tired shoulders of the Spanish people. Ganivet's *aboulia* links up with the pessimistic tone of the so-called "generation of '98", the "pulseless Spain" spoken of by a politician of the early twentieth century, compared with the "super-pulsation" referred to by another in June 1936. When analysed in the right perspective, both these—and other manifestations— may well only mean the strivings of a country to find its true self, to weather a stormy period of its history and to incorporate itself in modern Europe without losing its own special characteristics.

Nevertheless, *aboulia* existed in the sector of community which stood most in need of good health. Naturally Ganivet expected that the burden of the reconstruction would fall on "the intelligent and the disinterested", and almost immediately he laments "we have few examples of men possessed of a silent patriotism". In this phrase he laid his finger on the sore. One of the most depressing but least noted of the phenomena of this period is the absence of a genuine directing class. Much later Ortega y Gasset was to call attention to this, though from a different point of view. There are in Spain examples of great personalities—generally springing from the middle classes or the people—but in the traditional "ruling classes" there is an almost complete absence of direction and sense of duty. Attentive only to their privileges, they completely forgot their duties, remained divorced from the people and thus, betraying the country, betrayed their own interests. The clash between this selfishness and static disposition of those above and the impatience, logical but excessive, of those below, rendered impossible the liquidation of the nineteenth century and the normal working out of the problems of the present.

But in spite of all Ganivet is anything but pessimistic. This is what differentiates him from the majority of the generation of '98. "I have faith in the spiritual destiny of Spain." He believes that the nation can recover its health by means of a prudent régime and gradual but steady advance. "We have the main thing, the type of man we want. All that is needed is to see that he sets his hand to the work."

Realising that in Spain all theories are quickly transformed into weapons of combat, Ganivet declares himself in favour of what he terms "rounded" as opposed to "sharp-edged" ideas. His attempt to carry this out in the *Idearium* did not prevent others from using his ideas as weapons. From the time of the book's appearance the "two Spains" have claimed him as their supporter, and he has also suffered attacks from both sides. In 1925 his mortal remains were transferred from the cemetery at Riga to be reinterred in his native Granada. Under the pretext of rendering homage to his memory, the opportunity was taken for a protest against the dictatorship of Primo de Rivera. Someone acutely described the ceremony as a "manifestation of nonconformity". The Falange, lacking any philosophic content of its own, attempted to present Ganivet as a precursor of the "Movement", whilst its rivals inside Spain—the "traditionalists"—quoted him in support of their propaganda. The present revival of the *Idearium* inside Spain is echoed by the new editions, and new approaches to Ganivet, on the part of the Spanish exiles in Latin America.

Neither in the man nor in the book is there anything to justify the use of the *Idearium* for partisan purposes. Intellectually Ganivet is a typical product of his time. Influenced, like many of his contemporaries, by German philosophical schools, well-read in Renan and Tolstoi, with a solid background of Spanish culture, he exemplifies in many respects the spiritual inquietude which characterises the Europe of his day, and which in Spain had its most typical results in the work of Unamuno. Hence Ganivet's defence of Catholicism has nothing in it of fanaticism or intolerance. His conception of tradition has nothing to do with "traditionalist" political parties.

At the end of the nineteenth century Spanish thought was

again divided into two opposite bands: the Europeanisers and the traditionalists, or rather *casticistas*. In essence it was a continuation of the old struggle between Liberals and Absolutists, the same as is waged to-day between "Left" and "Right". Reason and unreason were apparent on both sides. For the former the root of all evil lay in the spiritual isolation of Spain from the rest of Europe. A bitter criticism of all Spanish values leads almost to a negation of Spain. For the latter the evil lies precisely in the appearance in Spain of all the "nefarious" political theories of the nineteenth century and in the neglect of the old Spanish tradition, which according to them was the supreme cause of Spanish greatness in past centuries. In this group there are also those for whom the term "tradition" has an exclusivist and class value. By tradition they mean the maintenance of the *status quo* with all their privileges and rights, and the denial of any trend of Spanish ideas opposed to their interests.

Between these two bands Ganivet, amongst others, took a middle course. He accepts all changes; he thinks they are both useful and necessary provided they are adapted to the realities and the idiosyncrasies of the country. There can and must be changes, but they must respect historical continuity and the inner soul of a nation—changes which occur with an imperceptibly slow tempo. "The most important philosophy of each nation", he writes, "is her own, even if it is inferior to foreign imitations." This leads him to the problem of Spanish Catholicism. "The weakness of Catholicism lies, not as is generally thought in the rigidity of its dogmas, but in the blunting effect produced on some nations, principally on Spain, by the systematic use of force." Against this use of force Ganivet raises a protest, not because of any anti-Catholicism, but because of the root that Catholicism had, and still has, in Spain. This is so clear to him that he cannot understand how liberty can be considered a potential danger, and he gives a wa ning that has not been heeded: "Force destroys not only dissident opinions, but the very faith it tries to protect."

Equally balanced is his interpretation of tradition. He thinks it would be difficult to build anything permanent in Spain unless it is based on the essence of tradition. But its essence must be clear to everybody: "What we have to take from tradition is what it gives or imposes upon us—the spirit." As to historic deeds or facts—"many are of no use, others even harmful", because "the past, though a powerful centre of resistance, is a weak source of activity".

Due to the very nature of the book, the author cannot fail to touch on the main Spanish problems—regionalism, agrarian reform, the Army, education, the Church—of which the solution is still to be found. The very fact that now and then Ganivet has been quoted by all parties, from the traditionalists to the typically Spanish anarchists, is a clear proof of his freedom from party dogmatism, and of his tacit acceptance of the good that is in each one of them. This political syncretism, so badly needed by Spain, helps him to see what should be the natural development of his country: "When all Spaniards, even at the sacrifice of theoretical convictions, accept a system of law fixed, indisputable and over a long period unchanged, and set themselves unanimously to labour at the task which interests us all, then it may be said that we have entered on a new historic period."

Spain is one of the countries about which most has been written since 1936. The Spanish Civil War roused as much passion outside as inside the country. It was soon evident that foreign elements were active in the Spanish ferment, that the peninsula was once again the battlefield of opposing "ideologies", and that consequently the struggle there was merely the rehearsal for the coming world conflict. Nevertheless, the international character rapidly acquired by the war in Spain had the effect abroad of producing a widespread confusion of the national character of that same war. Foreign political parties—Right and Left—fell over one another in their anxiety to interpret, according to their own preconceptions, the confused and varied ideologies existing in each one of the contending camps. They all overlooked the fact that foreign importations always produce in Spain a strange precipitate on contact with totally different realities and racial characteristics. Little attention is paid to this phenomenon in the multiplicity of recent writings on

Spain. This book, an attempt at a philosophical interpretation of Spanish history, may in spite of inconsistencies—
which are not as great as at first sight they appear to be—
offer the foreign reader a background of what is permanently
Spanish against which the realities of the day can be
projected and in harmony with which all changes must take
place.

Fifty years have passed since its publication. Once again
Spain is in the throes of another crisis. There are already
signs of a new epidemic of "interpretations", and not only by
Spaniards. Shortly after the publication of the *Idearium*
there was an exchange of open letters between Unamuno
and the author. The great Basque wrote: "Our capital sin
was, and still is, our unyielding character and our absurd
conception of unity." And Ganivet answered: "Sometimes
I think that the two great forces in Spain, the one that holds
her to the past and the one that rushes her forward, are
disjointed only because they do not *want* to understand one
another." Can any modern writer add anything to these
presentations of the old issues?

The translator of this book could very well have written
his own interpretation, but his interest in and love for Spain
made him choose the selfless task which lay at hand of
presenting to the English-speaking world the works of
several prominent Spaniards, amongst them these medita-
tions of one of the most original if tormented spirits of the
close of the nineteenth century.

R. M. NADAL.

§ A

THE idea has often occurred to me, when reflecting on the passion with which the dogma of the Virgin Birth has been defended in Spain, that beneath this doctrine there must lie some mystery linked up by hidden ways with the mystery of our national soul. That perhaps this doctrine is the symbol, and an admirable one, of our national existence, in which, after the long and painful labour of maternity, we find ourselves in old age still virgin in spirit. It is as if a woman, drawn as by irresistible vocation to a conventual, ascetic life, were married against her will and became a mother through duty, only to find at the end of her days that, surrounded by the children of her body, her soul remained apart, dedicated to the ideals of virginity.

When we examine the idealistic basis of Spain the moral, and to a certain extent the religious, element that we find to be most profound, forming as it were its foundation, is Stoicism. Not the brutal, heroic Stoicism of Cato, not the calm, majestic Stoicism of Marcus Aurelius, not the rigid, extreme Stoicism of Epictetus, but the natural, human Stoicism of Seneca. It is no matter of chance that Seneca is a son of Spain; he is a Spaniard by essence. Not an Andalusian; for when he was born the Vandals had not yet come to Spain; and had he been born later on, say in the Middle Ages, he would have been a son, not of Andalusia, but of Castile. The whole doctrine of Seneca may be summed up in this saying: Let nothing outside your own soul overcome you; amid all the chances of life, remember that you have within you a central, indestructible force; a diamond-hard axis, round which revolve the petty happenings which make up our daily existence; and whatever may fall to your lot of what men call prosperity or adversity, or even of those things that seem to tarnish with their touch, bear yourself so firm and resolute, that at least it may be said of you always: "Here is a man!"

This is Spanish; and so Spanish is it that Seneca had no need to invent it, it was discovered before him: he had only to take it and mould it into lasting shape, which is the way the true man of genius works. The spirit of Spain, rude and formless, does not cover its nakedness with elaborate drapery, it is content with the Senecan fig-leaf.

When as a student I read the works of Seneca I was left dazed and astounded, as one who, after the loss of sight or hearing, should suddenly and unexpectedly recover the lost sense, and find that objects, whose imagined sounds and colours previously floated confused in his mind, now come flooding forth to take on the consistency of real and tangible things.

Immense, immeasurable rather, is the part played by the Senecan philosophy in the religious and moral formation of Spain; in its customary law, in everyday arts and knowledge, in proverbs, maxims and sayings, and even in those branches of science with which Seneca was never concerned. For example, because this philosopher of ours had the inspiration, beyond all meed of praise, of taking his leave of life by the quiet, peaceful method of blood-letting, he has had as great an influence on our medical science as Hippocrates or Galen. Spain stands above all other nations by the number and excellence of its leeches. The supreme doctor of Germany is Doctor Faustus, and the supreme doctor of Spain is Doctor Sangredo, in spite of the existence of his famous professional rival, Doctor Pedro Recio de Tirteafuera. Never in the history of the human race do we meet with such a splendid example of unyielding stoicism as is afforded us by the endless series of undaunted leeches, who, century after century, have undertaken to ease the blood-pressure of Spaniards, sending numbers to the grave, it is true, but so purging the others of their excess as to allow them to live in relative peace and calm. And it may be that the discovery of the circulation of the blood by Servet, the one notable contribution of Spaniards to the practical sciences, owes its origin to Seneca and his crowd of followers.

Without attempting to discover subterranean connections between the doctrines of Seneca and Christian morals, one patent, undeniable relation may be established. Both are, as it were, the terminus of one evolution and the starting-point of another in a contrary direction; both meet and cross, like travellers coming from opposite ways and continuing their journey, each over the road already traversed by the other. The terminus of a rationalist philosophic evolution, such as the Greco-Roman, is reached when all possible solutions are exhausted: be they empirical or constructive, materialist or idealist, eclectic or synthetic, negative or sceptic. There then arises the Stoic moral, without other basis than virtue or self-respect. But that solution is only temporary, for very soon mankind, despising the power of mere reason, which leads to nothing positive, shuts its eyes and accepts a creed. The terminus of a theological evolution, as in the case of the Hebrews, must likewise be reached when all the historic solutions are exhausted, that is, all forms of action; a negative solution, what to-day we should call anarchist. Such was that foretold by the prophets. There must then arise a morality like the Christian one, which condemns action and, seeing in it the cause of human suffering, reconstructs human society on a basis of peace, self-sacrifice and love. But soon again mankind, disillusioned of faith, which tends to merely negative acts, turns back to reason, and starts a new evolution which displays itself not in action but in ideology.

Hence, the Christian moral, though logically derived from the Judaic religion, was a negative one for the Jews, since, by bringing to a close their religious evolution, it shut off the horizon of their hopes and condemned them to reclusion within a religious system now finished, perfected and consequently immutable. In the same way the Stoic moral, legitimately based on the one thing left standing by philosophy, on what persists even in periods of the greatest decadence, namely, the instinct of human dignity, was a negative one alike for Greeks and Romans, because, though based on an effort of the reason, it attempted to build up everything without the assistance of reason, by an act of blind adhesion which approached as near to faith as the

Christian moral did to reason. And so, by this natural concatenation, Christianity found the ground prepared for it by the Stoic moral, which had sown throughout the world noble, just, humanitarian ideas, but lacked the vital sap necessary to make them fructify. Nobility, justice, humanity, supported and protected by the reason alone, cannot, now or ever, overcome the lower passions, vile and animal, of the generality of mankind. In order to enchain the irresponsible power of the great, to tame the concentrated fury of impotence in the lowly, to soften somewhat the refined egoism of those in the middle scale, it is necessary to fuse them all together in the flames of a fire which, coming down from on high, builds up by destroying, and by consuming purifies.

Those who wonder at the rapid and apparently inexplicable propagation of Christianity should consider that, when paganism was destroyed by philosophy, and philosophy by the philosophers, there was no scope for anything but a belief which would take root, not in the form of symbols by then outworn, but in the form of a ray of idealism piercing and setting aflame. And those who are horror-struck at the bloody holocaust of innumerable martyrs should consider, that just as the death of Christ was a condition, prophetic, essential, necessary and complementary of the teaching of the Gospels, so likewise the martyrdom of many Christians was the one efficacious method of propagation. Without the sacrifice of Christ, He would have been just one more moral teacher; without the sacrifice of the martyrs, Christianity would have been one more moral system added to the many which have existed and now exist without any visible influence.

All religions, and in general all ideas have been, are and will be propagated in similar manner. They are like stones, which, falling into a pool, produce a circle of waves of varying extent, and of greater or less duration. Christianity fell from a great height, from Heaven, and, consequently, its waves have been so widespread and enduring. But the most remarkable thing in the propagation of Christianity was not its rapidity nor its intensity. Why should it be a matter of wonder that in different fields, ploughed, manured and sown with wheat, there should spring up simultaneously

many, infinite blades of corn? More wonderful, more strange
it is that, by means of skilful grafting, there should grow on
certain trees fruits which are natural to others, and that the
two saps, mingling and fusing, should delight the palate
with new and delicate flavours.

Such was the case with Christian morality grafted on to
the Gentile mind. While in appearance nothing more is
visible than a propagation of Christianity, in secret another
propagation was being carried out, that of Gentile philosophy, now Christianised. The point at which the grafting
was affected was the Stoic moral system. Thus in Spain, the
seat of the most logical form of Stoicism, not the most
perfect but the most human, the Senecan philosophy is so
intermingled with the Gospel that it may be said of our
Seneca, if not indeed that he has the "odour of sanctity",
at least that he has all the appearance of a Father of the
Church.

In Spain, then, as in all countries invaded by the Christian
idea, the spread of the Gospel is accompanied by a rational
endeavour to explain and complete it, but that endeavour
was not at the start, as it should have been, a creative effort,
but rather the work of rhapsodists. Instead of starting with
empirical theories related to the purity of the new faith, the
Christian philosophers of our western world, who, though
Christians, were living with blood inherited from their pagan
fathers, thought it more practical to bring into line with
Christianity the masterly teaching of the Hellenic school.
As they saw everything shaping into a perfect picture, fools
as they were (if I may be pardoned the bluntness) they
chose the best they found, the theories of the two leading
lights of Grecian wisdom: Plato and Aristotle.

Nevertheless, this evolution was not and could not be
identical in the different provinces of the Roman Empire,
for neither was the union such as to destroy the specific
character of each province, nor could that union be maintained long enough after the preaching of the Gospel to give
cohesion to the divergent tendencies which manifested
themselves on all sides. Leaving out of account the heresies
which attacked the unity of dogma and in the result produced great divisions in the Church, even in those countries

which preserved unchanged what was fundamental in the religion, there were divergences arising out of variety of temperaments which were gradually accentuated, in accordance with the historical changes which produced new, differentiating characteristics; and Spain was the country which created a Christianity special to itself, original as far as there is room for originality in Christianity.

Those historians who are fond of antithesis and contrast try to convince us that the body in which Christianity became incarnate was the Barbarians—"for new ideas, new men"—the Roman people, being decrepit with age, were incapable of understanding the new religion. The truth, on the contrary, is that this religion was destined not only to withdraw the savages from their savagery and the Barbarians from their barbarism; it was of far greater power: it availed to regenerate men who had attained to culture, men degraded but civilised. If the Barbarians had been able to move about freely they would in a short time have split up Christianity into numerous heresies, and would have ended by denaturalising it. For the Barbarians, when they came on the scene, were in a social condition analogous to that of the Greeks, some centuries before Homer; being Aryans, though backward in development, they had worked out a mythology with its gods and semi-divine heroes, and were prepared to set in motion the complicated stage machinery. Nothing was further removed, then, from their spirit and tendency than the spirit of Christianity. The action of the Barbarians was the material one of the breaking up of states; after destroying what perhaps there was no need to destroy, they became submerged in the peoples whom they were attempting to rule by force: they were caught in their own nets.

The exaltation of the Spanish Church under Visigoth rule is the work of the Barbarians; not, however, the result of their will, but of their impotence. Incapable of governing a people of higher culture, they resigned themselves to preserving the appearance of power, leaving effective power to more skilful hands. So that the principal part taken by the Visigoths in this matter was to take no part at all, and thus involuntarily to afford an opportunity for the Church to take possession of the main machinery of power and to establish in fact that Religious State which still subsists in our country. From this arose that metamorphosis of Christianity into Catholicism; that is, into a religion, universal, dominant, in actual possession of the temporal attributes of sovereignty. The downfall of the Visigoth power finds its explanation in this machinery of government; its domination was not destroyed by the African invaders, for they could not destroy what no longer existed. The theocratic power, which was afterwards to be of great value in the struggle against the Moors, was in the Gothic period the cause of the national ruin; because in the case of the Goths it was merely a head served by weak, unskilful arms, whereas during the Reconquest it was at the one time head and arms.

In a word, the Visigothic period, which for those who only attend to appearances is transcendental and decisive in the formation of our religious spirit, is to my mind only of external importance. During this period, it is true, religion acquires formidable social power, but shows itself rigid and solemn to excess. Religious sentiments do not become deeper or more energetic; the philosophy is scholastic philosophy in embryo, with no character of its own, and the extension of culture is, we may say, merely quantitative in result and therefore not of real importance. For the social influence of a school is not measured by the number of its disciples, nor the extent of its programmes, but by the superior, original minds it produces; just as the greatness of a nation is not measured by the density of its population or the extent of its territory, but by the magnitude and permanence of its action in history.

The most original and fruitful creation of our religious spirit takes its rise from the Moslem invasion. The spirit of Spain does not, as some think, become silent in order to leave the field clear for action; what it does is to speak through action. Thought may be expressed in very different ways, and its most beautiful mode of expression is not always in words. Whilst in the schools of Europe Christian philosophy was being atomised in sterile and at times ridiculous discussions, in our land it was being transformed into a permanent warfare, and as such sprang forth not from pen and ink, but amid the clash of arms and the rush of blood; it was not consigned to the tomes of a library, but enshrined in popular warlike poetry. Our *Summa*, theological and philosophical, is to be found in our *Romancero*.

And the great originality of this mode of expression lies in the fact that, springing as it did from the clash of two forces, it was to be a reflection of both. The Spaniards, when celebrating their exploits, did so in a Christian spirit, for it was through and with it that they fought; but the dress they gave to their concepts was to a large extent cut in Moorish fashion. The culture of the Moors was at that time reaching its zenith, and it was natural that it should have an influence on that of the Spaniards, were there not already a sufficient contact lasting over several centuries of warfare, which is often the most efficacious method of reciprocal influence between peoples. From that popular poetry, at once Christian and Moorish, with the Moorish element not devitalising the Christian, but rather heightening its tone, there sprang the two most marked tendencies in the religious spirit of Spain: mysticism, the exaltation of poetry; and fanaticism, the exaltation of action. Mysticism was, as it were, a sanctification of Moslem sensualism, and fanaticism a turning against ourselves, when the Reconquest was over, of the fury accumulated during eight centuries of strife. The same spirit that rose to the sublimest flights of thought created formidable and terrifying institutions; and when we wish to find something that will bring into strong relief our traditional character we have to resort, in apparent contradiction, to the *autos de fe* and to Saint Teresa's ecstasies of Divine Love. Compared with such original and vigorous creations, our doctrinal philosophy, imitated from the scholastics and pursued with much constancy, but little display of genius, loses a great deal of its value. It takes on the appearance of an effort of centralisation, if one might put it that way, of something out of harmony with our temperament; a creation of the Universal Church in order to maintain united, in a teaching complementary to dogma, the diverse social units subject to its supreme authority. It is not a matter of opposition, it is an inequality of force, and the Spanish spirit excels the external spirit; first, because

it is our own and, therefore, more suited to our genius, and
secondly, because it is more logical, more in agreement with
the original spirit of Christianity.

*   *   *

The movement towards conciliation in philosophy, begun
in Alexandria and continued up to the present time by the
scholastics, starts from an initial error which might be called
an error of perspective. This did not affect the essence of
the teaching, but in the course of time was to bring about
great confusion in philosophy. Instead of slowly building a
philosophy of their own, the new teachers furbished up the
philosophy of the Greeks, whose spirit was in antagonism to
the Christian spirit. Instead of soaring with the wings given
to them by faith, they crawled about the libraries; instead of
being Christian philosophers, they were philosophic
Christians; instead of creating out of their new spirit a new
philosophy, they wrote commentaries in a new spirit on
the old philosophy.

The greatest figure among the schoolmen, in the common
opinion, is Saint Thomas Aquinas; but Saint Thomas,
though he has the cut of an Aristotelian, is no Aristotle. His
philosophy is learned, prudent, foreseeing, even cautious;
it contains minute legislation, very useful for the ordered
life of the Church; but it is a "feminine" work: it lacks the
manly energy that stamps the work of the true creator. How
much more vigorous the figure of Saint Augustine, who,
without attempting to construct an encyclopædia of philosophy, establishes the City of God, no hollow organism like
the products of modern sociology, but something real which
functions, which lives!

The Christian spirit was not so much in need of seeking
support in minute classifications, in syllogisms, distinctions
and subtleties, as of penetrating into reality in order to
illuminate it with a new light, to point the way to new paths.
A Christian cosmology should be not a classification, nor a
description, but a canticle in which all created beings are
shown forth under a divine light, living with the one breath
of life and love, something in the style of the *Introduction to the*

Symbol of Faith of Fray Luis de Granada. A Christian psychology should not be over-concerned to describe so many organs, functions and operations as are conventionally assigned to our poor human soul, but rather to show us a soul in action, living as no other soul had lived before the preaching of the Gospel, a soul illumined and purified like that of Saint Teresa of Jesus.

The power of metaphor in the world is immense, and at times harmful. If we mix a certain quantity of wine with a certain quantity of water, we say that the mixture is wine because we take the part for the whole. If the mixture goes bad, we do not say this mixture has gone bad, but this wine has turned, and the blame is put upon the wine for what is the fault of the water. This is what happens with scholastic philosophy; it contains philosophy drawn from many authors, it is wine very much watered which has gone sour, which has turned, for ideas "turn" when they lose their force and influence over the life of men. But in spite of the failure, it is not to be thought that Christian philosophy is dead; one form of it is dead, but the principle survives and gives life to new forms, just as the human species dies in some men, and is born and preserved in others. The basis of the conciliation lies in ourselves; in actual fact we carry it within ourselves. Consequently, all of us, whether we like it or not, are scholastics in a certain sense. The Higher Criticism has divorced reason from faith; positivism has attempted to separate knowledge from reason: materialism has tried to destroy the very basis of knowledge. And they are all scholastics, after their fashion. If a system existed which denied human dignity to man and recommended him to adopt the posture of quadrupeds, it would be as scholastic as the preceding ones. For when they have completed their negative and destructive philosophical task, the inventors of such systems have either to cease being thinkers and become lunatics, or they must build up something to maintain at least external social order. And this act of affirmation is either an act of cowardice or it is an act of faith, or of submission to a common opinion which is the product of faith.

When Kant, with his profound and subtle analysis, arrives

at the last confines of philosophic nihilism, he reaches a point no more distant than that reached by the keen Grecian sophists; he does not proceed to the extremity of letting himself be run over by a cart rather than recognise the reality of sensual knowledge. What differentiates Kant from the Greek philosophers is that in addition to pure or negative reason, he admits practical or constructive reason; and this practical reason is simply pure reason, tamed by Christianity, pure reason overruled by the law of attraction to the collective opinion. The "categorical imperative", in appearance something intimate to ourselves, is merely a reflection in the depths of each spirit, of a social condition created by the Christian spirit. There is, then, no means of escape; we may withdraw as far as we please from the centre of ideas which rules over us; we may describe immense orbits, but round this eternal centre we shall ever be forced to revolve.

Nor have those who from Bacon up to our own times have striven to furbish up "new organs" of knowledge, to follow new methods and to found a purely realistic and practical science, succeeded in setting up a new planetary system. Their labours, if they have really exercised any influence on those inventions on which our century prides itself, may have been useful; they have furnished mankind with certain conveniences, not altogether disagreeable, such as the power of speedy travel, though, unfortunately, it only serves to bring us quicker to the same place we would reach by travelling slowly. But their value as ideas is nil, and instead of dethroning metaphysics, they have come to serve it and possibly to favour it; they wanted to be masters and they are hardly even slaves. The man who, despising faith and reason, devotes himself to experiment and discovers the telegraph or the telephone must not think he has destroyed "old ideas"; all he has done is to labour for their more rapid circulation, for their wider propagation.

I happened to be one day in the Antwerp Picture Gallery standing before (I think it was) the "Last Supper" of Jordaens, when I saw coming towards me my servant, a chubby, buxom Flemish woman, bringing me one of those checks they hand out in museums in exchange for sticks and umbrellas. The reader will easily guess that I must have left my house in fine weather; that it had come on to rain, an almost daily occurrence in those climes; and that my worthy handmaiden had been kind enough to bring me an umbrella. Such was the fact, but it also happened that when I left the museum it had stopped raining and I returned home with the umbrella under my arm. And an idea then occurred to me which has now come back to mind and seems to fit in here very well. I thought that in this commonplace happening I had played the part—through no merits of my own, but as a mere chance effect of perspective—of the perennial force of the idea that resides in us; and that my servant had unconsciously represented practical, experimental knowledge. I give all praise to those learned and far-seeing men who have brought us the telescope and the microscope, the railway and the steamboat, the telegraph and the telephone, the phonograph, the lightning conductor, electric light and X-rays; they all deserve gratitude for the pains they have been to, just as I was grateful to my servant for the trouble she had taken, in her goodness of heart, to bring me my umbrella. But I also affirm that whenever I succeed in raising myself even a palm's breadth above the commonplaces of daily life, and feel the warmth and light of some great, pure idea, all those splendid inventions serve me to naught.

In order that the Christian philosophy may not remain a conventional formula, that it may exercise a real influence on the life of men, it must be based on that same life; as is also the case with laws and with art. Cosmopolitan laws and art are mere summer clouds, and a universal philosophy, as scholasticism attempted to be, defeats its own purpose. To submit to the pressure of an unchanging set of ideas the life of different people, of diverse origin and history, can only lead to that system of ideas being transformed into a label, a signboard, proclaiming an apparent unity under which lie hidden the forces special to each people, ever ready to burst forth, and the more violently in proportion to the length of the period of enforced silence. The philosophy of most importance to each people is, then, its own, even though it be inferior to imitations from outside. What comes from

without is subject to change, a matter of fashion; what is
peculiar to the country is permanent, the foundation on
which all construction should rest, must rest, when the
artificial comes tottering to the ground.

Why should the world, and especially the world of to-day,
attach such great importance to the merely external? It
looks as if people were afraid of getting to the root of things.
We are obsessed by the mania for unification, and lacking
the repose necessary for leaving this task to time we hasten
to set up apparent unities, relying on the real or feigned
blindness of those who are present at our manipulations. If
I were fond of dilemmas, I should propose one, as a worthy
counterpart of the famous dilemma of Omar which reduced
to ashes the Library of Alexandria. It would run thus: either
men tend by nature to form a single homogeneous organism,
or they tend to accentuate the differences existing within the
various groups. If we hold that they tend towards unification, let us stop worrying and have patience and faith in our
idea. If we hold that they tend towards separation, let us
not shut our eyes to reality nor row against the stream. Of
course there will always be someone to maintain that there
is a third horn to the dilemma; that mankind is not really
going in any direction, and that there is need, from time to
time, of the appearance of a genius to guide. It is probable
that the man who believes this also believes that he himself
is the genius predestined to lead his fellows like a flock of
sheep. To such a solemn idiot it is needful to remark that he
simply does not know his fellow beings; that the men who
believe they have led other men have led mere bodies, not
souls; that souls are led only by divine spirits, and that for
centuries past the womb of humanity is barren and can give
birth to no new gods.

Such apparent, conventional unities cannot destroy the
real diversity of things; they serve only to conceal it. The
Reformation was merely the manifestation of the rebellion
latent in minds which perhaps were never really Christian;
which could not understand the true meaning of Christianity,
because they had not yet convinced themselves of the
importance of rational effort, and when proclaiming the
right of private judgment were as logical, after their fashion,

as the heirs of the Greco-Roman spirit when defending blind and absolute submission to faith. The Greek schismatic religion likewise started an apparent unity, in which the Slav peoples were submerged; the future will have something to say about this unity. It is of no avail that the political authority, armed with terrible powers and linked up with the ecclesiastical authority, should struggle to maintain the pretence. Anyone who comes in contact with the Russian people will observe the unrest which precedes the explosion, the universal desire to break through the thick crust of Byzantine religion which imprisons natural forces and prevents them being manifested in their purity and spontaneity. In our days there is feverish toil to convert the African negro; it is possible that we may shortly be told that they are all now catechised. It is also possible that after some centuries they may be worshipping gross divinities not greatly superior to the fetishes they now adore, and living again in conformity with their native customs.

True Christianity, not as a philanthropic aspiration in favour of inferior races, but as a consciously professed belief, is unsuited to primitive peoples, and only takes root in them when accompanied by the permanent action of a superior race. That is to say, when the primitive people is mingled by common life or intermarriage with a civilised people which rules it and educates it, as happened with the races discovered and subjugated by Spain. This idea is not in contradiction with the universality or catholicity of Christianity. All men are mortal, and yet if we were asked as to the possibility of all the inhabitants of a city dying at the same time, we should deny it, basing our denial on what might be termed "instinctive experience", a kind of certainty which Balmes has analysed with great precision. And if in spite of this the abnormal fact were to present itself of the simultaneous death of an entire population, we should still not admit of the actual occurrence of "simultaneous dying", but should explain the anomaly by an exceptional, extraordinary cause: an epidemic, for example. In the same way, all men are capable of being catechised, but not all at the same time. When we see, in the beginning of Christianity, peoples converted *en masse*, we attribute it to an exceptional cause, the state of prostration of thought at which the Greco-Roman mind had arrived.

It would then be most fruitful, and nowise dangerous, to break up philosophic unity. The Spanish spirit has been submitted to the most formidable pressure ever devised by the most exclusive fanaticism, and this spirit, instead of rebelling, has recognised itself as both judge and accused, as both victim and executioner, and has by spontaneous effort gone much further than the point to which coercion would have forced it. We have the history of heterodoxy in Spain written by Menéndez y Pelayo, a Spaniard of such wide and generous judgment as to be capable of doing strict justice to the most hardened heretics, if he had been able to meet with any in his investigations. But there is no danger; in Spain there is not a heretic that rises a few inches from the ground. If anyone has tried to be a heretic, he has wasted his time; nobody has paid any attention to him. If in many aspects of life man has need of the help of society, in the formation of sects this is so decisive, that the importance of religious nonconformity is to be measured not so much by its doctrinal basis, as by the number of its adherents. Spain is interfused with its religious ideal, and however many the sectaries who should attempt to "decatholicise" it, they would only succeed in scratching the surface of the nation.

But after several centuries of silence, men have become afraid of the human voice, and lack the skill to appreciate words at their true value, not by the amount of noise they make. Hardly is a little liberty allowed to restless, undisciplined spirits, when a deep anxiety supervenes. People will not realise that the importance of what is said lies not so much in the actual matter spoken of, as in the excitement produced in those listening. Accustomed as they are to maintain unity of doctrine by means of force, they find it hard now to struggle to maintain it by an intellectual effort. As if it were not true that force destroys, together with the dissident opinions, the very faith it claims to defend! One of the errors which, with most appearance of truth, are in circulation to-day, is that the nations who accepted the Reformation have succeeded in acquiring a higher culture, greater prosperity, wider political influence, than those that remained faithful to Catholicism. I have lived several years in Belgium, and I can affirm that it is a nation as advanced as any other in all that order of things in which civilisation is held to consist (and in which unfortunately more importance is attached to railways than to works of art); and Belgium is a Catholic nation, more Catholic at bottom than Spain. But in Belgium there are other creeds, and there are besides strong anti-Catholic movements; the Catholics have to be on the alert, they have to struggle and they do struggle with as much ardour as in the days of the Duke of Alba.

The weakness of Catholicism lies, not as is thought, in the rigidity of its dogmas, but in the blunting effect produced on some nations, principally on Spain, by the systematic use of force. Anything that is built up in Spain on national lines should rest on the corner-stones of tradition. This is the logical, the noble thing, for having ruined ourselves in the defence of Catholicism, there could be no greater infamy than to betray our forefathers, and to add to the sorrow of a defeat, possibly only a transitory one, the humiliation of yielding to the influence of the ideas of our conquerors. But all the more for this being so clear, freedom should inspire no alarm. To-day we can no longer have heresies, for the growth of publicity, while increasing the power of diffusion of ideas, takes from them that intensity and heat which are needed for them to burn themselves in and give rise to real sects. Those who set out to be reformers can create nothing durable; they soon suffer disillusionment and end by accepting public office or paid employment. And these rewards are not unreasonable, for they recompense them for having done useful service to the nation; for having excited and stirred up genuinely national energies which had lain dormant. One might say of such men that they are like spices, which cannot be eaten as a meal, but are most useful when employed by a skilful cook. If there were some way of introducing into Spain a few salaried Freethinkers and a sprinkling of hired Protestants, perhaps the difficulty might be met without injury to the feelings of Spaniards; but if this be not possible, the only solution is to allow such groups to be formed at home, to tolerate and even, if necessary, to pay them.

When I was a child I read the hair-raising story of what
happened, in one of those countries bordering on the North
Pole, to a man who was travelling in a sleigh with five of his
children. The unfortunate traveller was attacked by a band
of ravenous wolves, who with fearsome yells gradually drew
nearer, till they flung themselves on the horses drawing the
sleigh.   In this desperate situation the distracted father
conceived a terrible project. Catching up one of his children,
the youngest, he threw it to the wolves, and whilst these, in
their fury, fought for the prey, he madly continued his
journey till he arrived at a place of protection and shelter.
Spain should do as that savage and loving parent; not
without reason is it the fatherland of Guzmán el Bueno, who
allowed his son to be beheaded before his eyes, under the
walls of Tarifa.   There are sentimental souls who will of
course say that the remedy is too brutal; but, faced with the
spiritual ruin of Spain, one must put a stone in the place of
one's heart, and even a million Spaniards must be thrown to
the wolves, unless we are all to go to the dogs.

*   *   *

The problem most difficult of solution in psychology, the
one that has defeated the most clear-sighted of investigators,
is that of linking in a logical chain our internal experience
with external phenomena.   There are psychologists who
construct perilous ideologies, elevating into general principles
the particular facts they observe in their own minds. There
are others who build up baseless phenomenologies by a co-
ordination of purely objective observations. And there are
some so keen-visioned as to fuse both these processes and to
explain what they observe in the rest of mankind by similar
happenings which they discover within themselves. And the
result is always uncertain, for at times two psychologically
identical subjects display antagonistic tendencies, and two
opposed subjects assume in real life identical appearances.
If we take as a type the misanthropist, it may happen that
in real life we meet him transformed now into an ascetic,
now into a demagogue. The essential psychological character
is the same—a man lacking in sentimental appetite, an

intransigent who lives isolated from the world around, like a ship that has lost its anchors and cannot make the port. And yet this man is equally suited for living in a monastery cell or for stirring up masses of people, sowing ideas which, by reason of their disassociation from the common ideas, are bound of necessity to be dissolvent.

To my mind, two natures so unlike as those of À Kempis and Proudhon are psychologically identical; the one thinks in silence, the other in the tumult of the crowd. But both are solitary thinkers, both have an equally negative concept of life; though in one case this is corrected and sweetened by faith, in the other it is exasperated and converted into a weapon of destruction. Contrariwise, two natures to all appearance similar, like À Kempis and Luis de Granada, are in reality diametrically opposed: À Kempis is elevated to asceticism through abstractions; his is an ontological mind; unsupported by abstractions he falls into lifeless, arid prose. Fray Luis rises to mysticism, supported by his wonderful knowledge of reality, his positive love for humanity; his mind is a realistic one, his thoughts are human thoughts. Of the one we might say that he is a weak lymphatic soul, of the other that he is robust and full-blooded.

In like manner, when we study the psychological structure of a country it is not sufficient to portray the external mechanism, nor is it prudent to find an explanation in a fantastic ideology; we must go deeper and search out in the reality of things that irreducible nucleus to which are attached the elements which in the course of time transform the physiognomy of the country. And as always when we dig deep we come upon the one thing that for us is permanent—the soil, that nucleus is to be found in the "territorial spirit". Religion, deep as it is, is not the deepest thing in a nation. Religion may change, whereas the territorial spirit persists, for geological changes occur at such rare intervals that various civilisations are born and die without any perceptible change being observed in the soil. Hence, if our investigations be limited to discovering the religious, the artistic, the juridical spirit, it may happen that we shall discover only externals, and shall deduce what look like analogies, where, if the generating principle be attended to, marked oppositions are found to exist.

The spiritual evolution of Spain is explained only when we place in contrast all the external facts of its history with the permanent, invariable spirit which the land creates, infuses and maintains in us. Just as there are continents, peninsulas and islands, so there are continental, peninsular and insular spirits. Territories have a national character which depends on the thickness and composition of their mass, and a character of relation which arises from their respective positions; relations of attraction, dependence or opposition. An island looks for support to the continent of which it is a kind of annexe, or reacts against that continent if its own strength allows it. A peninsula does not seek support, being of its nature already firmly fixed, and it reacts against the continent the more violently the further it is from continental centre. A continent is a mass in static equilibrium, forming a focus of permanent attraction. The spiritual evolution is more rapid in islands than in peninsulas, in these more than in continents, on the littoral more than in the interior. The evolution of a territory or of the individuals occupying it is in direct ratio to the distance from the centre of the territorial units, because distance provokes, together with the movement of reaction, another corresponding movement of spiritual impetus.

Comparing now the specific characters assumed in the different social groups by the inherent relations between their territories, we observe that in continental peoples the characteristic is that of resistance, in peninsular that of independence, in insular that of aggression. The general principle is the same: self-preservation, but the continental groups having frequent, necessary interrelations, trust to the spirit of resistance. The peninsular, living more isolated, though not exempt from attack and invasion, as they do not need a permanent defensive organisation, but rather one of union in case of danger, trust to the spirit of independence, which is exalted by aggression. The insular, living in isolated territory with fixed, invariable limits, and consequently less exposed to invasion, find themselves impelled, when necessity for action urges, to become aggressors. And it must not be thought that social groups need to have geographical knowledge in order to recognise the characteristic of their territory; accumulated historic experience furnishes them with perfect knowledge thereof. The islander knows that his surest defence lies in his isolation; he may submit to outside domination if he lacks the strength to preserve his independence; but in actual fact he is independent, and he furthermore knows that the force of characterisation in his insular soil is so great that, if alien elements are introduced into it, it is not long before they acquire this feeling of autonomy. On the other hand, the continental does not put his trust in the soil, since this does not offer him sufficient security; rather does he develop the spirit of resistance. He may be subdued, but relying on the strength of his specific character, on his passivity, he will retain his integrity in the midst of his conquerors. Finally, the peninsular likewise knows the weak spot of his territory, because through it he has always seen the invader enter; but, as through lack of constant relations with other races no spirit of resistance and foresight has been formed, he yields easily before the invader, struggles round his own homestead for independence, and if he is conquered intermingles with the invader more easily than does the continental.

When the territorial spirit is not yet formed, its place is taken by the political spirit, the sense of citizenship. When this has taken shape, it is akin to the insular spirit, for the man who lives in an enclosed and walled space thinks that it forms a separate unit of territory. Rome and Carthage were insular cities, their aggressive power was as great as their power of resistance small. Carthage succumbed to an attack from Rome, and Rome had been shortly before on the point of being crushed by the armies of Carthage.

The typical insular nation is England, and the history of England, from the time of its constitution as a nation, is one long aggression. Her attacks do not take the same form as those of the continental nations; they are premeditated and certain as those of the tiger which lies in wait before leaping at its prey. And this is not an act of will; it arises from the very nature of the territory; from the necessity of keeping up great maritime forces and the facility these give for isolated aggressions, against which all foresight and caution are useless. "I should like to see", wrote Cobden, "a map of the world with red marks in all those spots where the English have fought a battle; it would be evident that, in contrast with other peoples, the English have been fighting for seven centuries against foreign forces everywhere except in England. Is a single word more needed to prove that we are the most aggressive country in the world?" To this we might add that if England were to fight on her own soil, she would be more easily defeated than any other nation. "Had it not been for the disaster to the Armada, had the Spanish regiments set foot in England," says Macaulay, "we should have had a repetition of the tremendous disaster that befell Rome when Hannibal invaded Italy." Macaulay based this assertion on the military superiority of the Spanish soldiers, but it might be more accurate to say that England had and has within itself the cause of her weakness in a war of resistance; just as the impunity which she has always enjoyed is to be explained by the absence on the Continent of the conditions necessary for aggressive warfare, in the sense here given to the word aggression.

If we take France as an example of a continental nation, we shall find that in her the dominant feeling is the patriotic. In Spain, as from the very fact that we are almost an island, we look on ourselves as isolated, we concentrate our attention on the point whence attack may come. From this concentration arises the feeling of independence; we are almost independent and we wish to be so entirely. Whereas France, which has common frontiers with several nations, cannot conceive of her territory as isolated; she therefore exalts the idea of "*la patrie*", more effective to maintain cohesion, in times both of peace and of war, for in continental countries peace is not a period of repose, but a milder form of warfare, the struggle for intellectual predominance.

The French wars have always been frontier wars, defensive or offensive, but which always fit in with the traditional standpoint formed by the logic of history. The early years of the Revolution were merely defensive wars or wars for the diffusion of an ideal; aggression does not begin until the appearance of Napoleon, who was not only a foreigner who knew France in purely objective fashion and used it as an instrument to further his ambition (as Taine has maintained and proved), but who was also an islander, was in fact an island which threw itself upon the continent. If we study on a military map the strategy employed in the Napoleonic wars (with reason are they called Napoleonic and not French), we shall realise that Napoleon moved his armies as if they were naval squadrons; his wars are land wars in fact, but sea wars in conception. Hence the confusion of Europe, not accustomed to this kind of warfare. Europe struggled against Napoleon is every way in which it is possible to struggle: Spain, by a war of independence, England by isolated and sure attacks, the Continent by resistance, and finally, Russia by retreat. And to my mind Napoleon could have, by concentrating all his forces, attacked and destroyed England and perhaps subjugated Spain, but he would never have been able to triumph over the passive resistance of Russia. The spirit of Napoleon leaves such a strongly marked impression on France that it reappears in the Second Empire in the form of absurd aggressions contrary to France's interests. It even persists in the Third Republic in a still more degenerate form, that of colonial conquests, carried out in the name of a nation which is not a coloniser, which cannot advance beyond political domination—the protectorate, because of its people's repugnance to leaving the soil of the mother country.

Spain is a peninsula, more strictly "the peninsula", for no other approaches nearer to being an island than ours. The Pyrenees are both an isthmus and a wall; they do not prevent invasions, but they isolate us and allow us to preserve our independent character. In reality, we have always thought ourselves islanders, and perhaps this error may explain many anomalies in our history. We are an island situated at the meeting-place of two continents, and if ideally there is no isthmus, historically there are two: the Pyrenees and the Straits; we are a "house with two doors", and, consequently, "difficult to guard". Now, as it has been our unvarying policy to leave them both open, for fear lest the forces appointed to guard them should turn against ourselves, our country has been converted into a sort of international park, where all peoples and races have come to amuse themselves whenever they thought fit; our history is an interminable series of invasions and expulsions, a permanent war of independence.

But just as there are nations which have fought only on their own soil or in the neighbourhood of their frontiers, and others which have fought only on foreign territory, our nation has fought on all sides, and this fact, which seems to give the lie to what I have said about our territorial spirit, deserves an explanation. If by nature we are not aggressive, how are we to understand our modern history, where Spain, hardly constituted into a nation, shows herself warlike and conquering? Can this arise from the error before mentioned, from our thinking ourselves an island in spite of the stern warning given us by our delicate geographical position? I believe that this spirit of aggression does exist, but that it has been merely a transformation of our spirit of independence, and is bound to disappear with the causes that brought about this transformation.

A fact which at first sight seems inexplicable, the prolonged duration of the Moslem power in Spain, discovers for us the cause—there can be no other—of this strange transformation. Just as the existence of Turkey-in-Europe is explained, not by the innate vitality of the Turkish people, but by the rivalry of the Great Powers, unable to restrain their susceptibilities and suspicions, so likewise the existence of the Hispano-Moorish domination in its long period of decline rested mainly on the jealousy of the different Christian kingdoms. They wish to complete the Reconquest, but they fear what will follow after; they labour for the triumph of Christianity, but they do not overlook one important point: the preservation of the independence of the different parcels of the territory and the charter rights. Hence the absurd policy of the constant partition of kingdoms; inspired, not by paternal affection (for I have an idea that the kings of the Middle Ages were more hard-hearted than those of to-day), but by the demands of the different regions themselves, and even of the towns, who insisted on standing up for their own rights. Every advance made is followed by a halt for reflection; all look sideways at one another, compare and measure one another to see if one has grown a bit more and to chop off his head to bring him to the same level. Rare

are the periods in which, through the simultaneous appearance as governors of men of large ideas, equality is sought by struggle against the foe, by rivalry in ardour and energy. The lesser States, shut in on themselves and removed from the scene of the strife, either formed alliances or sought foreign help. Those whose frontiers remained exposed, as was the case in the latter period with Portugal, Castile and Aragon, strove to maintain the balance of power.

Nevertheless, this balance was bound to be upset, and it was at last clearly seen that Castile, by reason of its central position, was taking on its shoulders the main part of the work of Reconquest. As the future preponderance of Castile was a menace to the independence of the rest, there arose spontaneously, as a flowering of our territorial spirit, the idea of seeking outside Spanish soil the force required in order to be independent in Spain. Portugal, an Atlantic State, is transformed into a seafaring nation and turns its eyes towards the African continent. Aragon, Catalonia and Valencia, a Mediterranean State, finds its support in the Mediterranean and in Italy. In this way is born the "conquistador" spirit in Spain, distinguished from that of other peoples in that, whereas the rest undertake conquests when they have an excess of strength, Spain does so when lacking in strength, and precisely in order to gain it. It was in this manner that we became the "conquistadores" of the legends, the terrible falcons or eaglets of the famous sonnet "Les Trophées" of the Hispano-French poet, José María de Heredia.

The conquistador spirit is born in the west and east of Spain earlier than in the centre, in Castile, which afterwards monopolises it; and in each region it takes on a different character, imposed by the nature of the conquests. In Portugal the conquerors are navigators and discoverers, but not from a spirit of curiosity, for it is the desire of dominion that impels them. In Catalonia and Aragon we meet traces of the typical conqueror, especially in the celebrated expedition against Turks and Greeks, but the predominant feature is conquest based on politics and diplomacy. "The incorporation of Navarre to the Crown of Spain", Castelar has said, "is a chapter out of Machiavelli." Ferdinand the

Catholic is no improvised diplomat, he is a master formed in the Italian school, much more astute than Machiavelli, who at bottom (I am not being ironical) was a decent sort, as we would say to-day, an excellent patriot, enthusiastic for the idea of United Italy, desirous that his country should be great and powerful as the rest, and convinced that his ideal could not be realised by means other than those employed by his adversaries. Machiavelli has earned the infamy attached to crooked and treacherous notions for having written down and systematised what in his time was practised by princes looked upon as most Christian. The conquerors from the eastern part of Spain were then the more "civilised", on account of the medium to which they had to adapt themselves. In Italy we learned of necessity to be skilled diplomatists, and in Italy we transformed the warriors of the siege of Granada into an army organised in the most perfect form that our weak organised powers have been able to compass.

In Castile, the conquering spirit has its origin in the spirit of rivalry, supported by religion. The natural tendency of Castile was to carry forward on African soil the struggle against the Moslem power, the renewal of whose offensive might be feared. But Columbus interposed and the forces that should have gone to Africa were transferred to America. The political organisation given to the country by the Catholic kings required as a natural complement an intellectual restoration, to give to the works of the mind wider scope in the national life, and a material restoration of the forces of the country impoverished by warfare. But both these undertakings demanded great constancy and great effort. The first was brilliantly initiated, for the impulse came from the sovereigns and the talented men they knew how to gather round them. But the second, a matter of hands rather than of head, of perspiration rather than of perspicacity, was to depend upon the workers of the population; and these, not feeling very much disposed to take up the task, welcomed with joy the tidings of a new-found world, which attracted and seduced like some form of magic. And laying down the prosaic instruments of toil, as many as could started off in search of personal independence, as represented by "gold";

not gold earned in industry or commerce, but gold in the natural state: nuggets.

Thus it comes about that the spirit of aggression so generally attributed to us is, as I have said, merely a transformation of the territorial spirit. Through its long duration it has come to acquire the character of a distinctive mark of our race, but it has not really imposed itself on us, and is bound to disappear when the last echoes of the policy which gave rise to it are extinguished. In the history of Spain we meet with only one attempt at real aggression: the despatch of the Armada against England. Yet it is well known that this enterprise, with its disastrous and quite logical issue, was not our exclusive work. We furnished the arm, but not the idea; the political or religious interests of a nation do not include the whole of its intimate thought. An examination of the documents relating to Papal diplomacy in Spain (of which a careful study has been made by a Spanish writer, D. Ricardo de Hinojosa) makes it plain that if Spain entertained for a moment the notion of attacking England, the protector and supporter of the revolted Flemings, that idea was encouraged, supported, revived and subventioned by the Church of Rome, with even greater urgency than was employed in setting up the League against the Turks, which in fact answered to a nobler inspiration, that of defence against a violent power, ever on the increase, and a danger to the interests of all Europe.

In our internal history, full as it unfortunately is of civil strife, there are to be found no wars of aggression, but only struggles for independence. Union is brought about peacefully by virtue of marriage or hereditary right; in this way were joined Aragon and Catalonia, Castile and Aragon, Spain and Portugal. War appears only when the separation takes place; on one side the struggle is for independence, on the other for the maintenance of unity, that is to say, of established political legality; there is consequently no aggression. A fact such as the occupation of Gibraltar by England, without right or precedent to justify it, a matter of calculation and convenience, has no parallel in our history.

*   *   *

The terms "warlike spirit" and "military spirit" are generally employed indifferently, and yet I know none more opposed to each other. A first glance will show that the warlike spirit is spontaneous, the military spirit a matter of taking thought; one resides in the man, the other in society; one is an effort directed against organisation, the other derived from organisation. A man armed to the teeth advertises his weakness if not his cowardice; a man who fights unarmed makes it clear that he has absolute confidence in his own valour. A country which relies on its native forces disdains militarism; a country which doubts its security puts all its trust in barracks. Spain is of its essence, for its territorial spirit so demands, a warlike, not a military nation.

Open a history of Spain at any page and we shall constantly meet with the same fact: a people which struggles without organisation. In the Roman period we know that Numantia preferred to perish rather than yield. What we do not know is who was the leader there, and we are almost sure that there was no leader. We look for armies and we find only guerrilla bands, the outstanding figure being not a regular leader, king or kinglet, but Viriatus, a guerrilla chief. During the Reconquest, among so many kings, some wise, some even saints, the national figure is the Cid, an ambulatory king, a guerrilla chief in business on his own account. The first act that announces the future predominance of Castile does not proceed from a king, but from the Cid when he undertakes the conquest of Valencia, intercepting the advance of Catalonia and Aragon. No matter that the conquest was not final: the intention, the impetus, was enough, and accordingly the Castilian people are not in error when they exalt the figure of the Cid high above their kings. When the fighting men seek a support in their religion, they are not content with invoking divine assistance; they transform Saint James into a warrior, not a general, be it noted, but a simple cavalry soldier. And this is not a matter exclusively of religion, of hatred of the infidel, for in our own century, against French Christians, Aragon transforms Our Lady of the Pillar into captain of the Aragonese troops.

When the force of circumstances oblige us to intervene in European affairs, the warrior is changed into the man-at-arms, but our military creations are not complicated organisms, they are the company and the regiment. To offer Europe a military figure of the first order, we have to turn to a mere captain, the Great Captain, the creator of our army in the Italian campaigns. And the special excellence of Gonzalo de Córdoba lay in the fact, as I pointed out was the case with Seneca, that he invented nothing, that he simply gave form to our already existing ideas. There were great armies at the period, and the Great Captain created tactics for those which were numerically smaller, a defensive combined with rapid movements and isolated attacks; in other words, guerrilla tactics, an infallible means for breaking enemy cohesion, dividing it and defeating it, when that enemy confides for success in a single head and deadens the initiative of secondary, free-moving sectors.

No change was needed to carry out our American enterprises, and the conquistadores, in their fighting capacity, were genuine *guerrilleros*, from the highest to the lowest of them, not excepting Hernán Cortes. This is the reason why Europe has never understood them, has compared them to bandits. Hundreds of times, since I have been living out of Spain, I have heard the everlasting accusation, made by learned and ignorant, even by poets, who generally adopt a less narrow standard in judging human affairs. Heine, in his *Romancero*, in the gloomy legend of "Vitzliputzli", also calls Hernán Cortes "a captain of bandits". And instead of getting indignant at this, I think the sensible thing is to say that they do not understand our conquistadores, because they have never been able to produce such themselves.

Holland imitated the policy of Portugal and sought in colonisation the strength which the smallness of its territory did not afford it in order to maintain its independence on the Continent. But Holland already possessed other much more perfect means of action, and as furthermore her spirit was a different one, her colonisation was changed into a commercial enterprise, into something useful, practical, no doubt, but not so noble. And colonisation, thus understood, passed from the Continent to England, which was then to acquire colonial supremacy in the world; though it might be more exact to say that it passed not to England, but to Scotland, the Scots, not the English, being the pioneers. In our days, Belgium, or rather the King of the Belgians, has initiated the same policy (which may prove a dangerous one if, withdrawing the country from its neutrality, it should leave it without means to support by its own efforts what to-day is supported by the agreement of the Powers). But this policy is likewise based on commerce and on regular military action, not on the spirit of the conquistador, for we cannot give that name to those who serve a brief period in a colony in order to obtain honours or riches, but only to those who conquer, as it were, through necessity, spontaneously, from a natural impulse towards independence, without other purpose than to show forth the grandeur hidden under their apparent pettiness. And equally much a conquistador as Cortes or Pizarro is Cervantes, prisoner in Algiers and involved in a rising on behalf of Spain, and Saint Ignatius of Loyola, another obscure soldier who with a handful of men undertakes the conquest of the spiritual world. When Europe, therefore, accustomed to the regular progress of warfare and commerce, sees a few adventurers launch out on the conquest of a large territory, being unable or unwilling to understand the ideal which inspires them, she regards them as highwaymen, and interprets the cruelties committed by them not as incidents of warfare, but as a revelation of vile, bloodthirsty instincts. She does not consider that, were it not for those misjudged heroes, of whom one might say that they broke the soil of the colonial world, there could not have come after them the sowers and the reapers, those who, not content with winning the material results of others' labour, claim for themselves all the glory.

Such errors of judgment are due to the systematic hypocrisy in which we all take refuge to-day, the voluntary blindness from which we all suffer. We link up effect with cause, only when these are already naturally connected and there is no way of separating them. An army fighting with long-range weapons, with quick-firing machine-guns and cannons of huge calibre, is a glorious army, though it leaves the field strewn with corpses; and if the corpses are of negroes, it is denied that there are any corpses. A soldier who fights hand-to-hand and kills his enemy with a bayonet-thrust is beginning to seem to us rather brutal; a man not in uniform who fights and slays is an assassin. We pay no heed to the act, it is the appearance to which we give attention.

Our society despises and abuses the money-lender; belauds and ennobles the financier. Why? Because the money-lender comes into direct contact with his customers, whereas the financier works on a large scale, making great use of telegraph and telephone. We are annoyed with the money-lender for charging an excessive rate of interest, because the victim knows the wrongdoer, and when he complains tells us the usurer's name. But we marvel and admire when the stock-jobber makes a million in a smart deal, because his victims do not know him, and as they sink to ruin, perhaps to suicide, cannot name the man who has played on their stupidity or their ignorance.

I have lived in countries where credit is admirably organised, where there is hardly any idle capital, for it is almost all in hands that are making it fructify. There are most varied schemes by which the workers may save, and earn interest on a shilling upward, by which children may start saving with a penny stamp, so that from childhood they may begin to acquire habits of economy. This is all to the good. But I have never lived in a country where, in a case of need, a poor family (there are such everywhere) can get more service out of an old shirt or a pair of worn pants than in Spain. Those people excel us in the negative aspect of credit, that of collecting; they are far inferior in its positive aspect, that of giving. Our credit again is organised guerrilla-fashion, with money-lenders as its chiefs. Their action is individual, and consequently, as we have seen, irritant. But their power of evil is restricted by their narrow field of operations; the wider this stretches, the greater the extent of their enterprises, till they reach a colossal stage, such as we refer to as "the wonders of finance". But the evil increases in the same proportion, and the resulting catastrophes are likewise marvellous and colossal.

I am not going to say absolutely that one is better than the other; the only thing one can say absolutely is that both are bad. I have no liking for property, individual or collective, but I understand it when it is based on affection. A man who owns a house, and loves it because in it he was born and hopes to die, is a useful proprietor. A man who builds houses and owns them only until he can sell them at a profit is a mischievous proprietor, because if not prevented he is quite capable of building them so badly that they will fall down and crush the tenants. All modern progress is insecure, because it is based not on ideas, but on the destruction of immovable, to the benefit of movable, property. This latter, which no longer serves merely to attend to the needs of existence, and which instead of being ruled by justice is ruled by strategy, is bound to disappear without leaving a trace, even as disappeared the brutal empires of the Medes and the Persians.

Our contempt for manual labour increases from day to day, and nevertheless in it lies our salvation. It alone can excite the sentiment of brotherhood, which demands the contact of men one with another. Thus, "civilised" warfare, which seems nobler because it sets a distance between those who kill and those who are slain, is profoundly selfish and savage, for it prevents any display of compassion. The man who fights from afar kills every time he hits his mark; the man who fights hand-to-hand sometimes kills, and sometimes takes pity and spares. The Spanish are looked upon as harsh and cruel fighters, and they may well be those who have afforded most examples of compassion and magnanimity, not because they are in themselves more magnanimous and more compassionate, but because they have always fought at close quarters with the enemy.

To make use of an everyday and therefore more forcible example, I shall compare the small bootmaker with the boot-manufacturer. If I ask which of the two is more praiseworthy in his profession, I shall be told that the manufacturer is, because he works on a large scale with greater exactness and elegance and possibly at a lower price. I am all for the small bootmaker, because he works only for a few customers and comes to know their feet and to look upon these feet as his personal concern. When he makes a pair of boots, he is not simply gaining a livelihood, he goes to all the pains he can to ensure that the boots fit the feet perfectly, or at any rate comfortably, and this good intention of his is sufficient to raise him in my eyes far above the manufacturer, who looks only to his profits, and far above the employee, who looks only to his wages. We arrive, then, at the same conclusion as when we were discussing the house-owner: there is a socially useful worker, who loves his work, and there is a mischievous one, who works only from a utilitarian instinct. It is not only the head that tells me this; when I consider the case of the bootmaker, it seems to me that even our feet would take the part of the almost disappearing descendants of Saint Crispin, who certainly never worked in a factory, and had he been a manufacturer would never have been a saint.

Whenever in Spain there presents itself a conflict which requires for its solution the intervention of armed force, we witness the spectacle of the insubordination of all social classes, anxious to take on themselves the functions of the State, in which they have no absolute confidence, and to assume to themselves the conduct of the struggle. Sensible men harshly condemn all such attempts; they cry out against the unbalanced mind of the country and demand little less than solemn, religious silence while the army fulfils its mission undisturbed. This is logical, this is scientific, but it is not Spanish. If it were possible to destroy all the anomalies in our character, it would be necessary at once to substitute for them a militarism as unbridled as that which to-day oppresses the nations of the Continent. When the whole world is increasing its military power in formidable fashion, two countries alone hold back. England, traditionally opposed to large armies, possesses only an army organised in accordance with her own ideas and suited to the needs of her policy. Spain entrusts the safeguarding of her independence to the territorial spirit, counting on sufficient forces to maintain internal order; she has not even a colonial army, in spite of being a colonial power. And it may be that the two nations which can view the future with most security are Spain and England, because the one finds her most solid support in her national character and her isolation, and the other in her insular position and her naval forces.

If, then, it were possible to destroy our territorial spirit

and to entrust our interests to a large and disciplined army,
our independence which is to-day unquestioned would be
constantly menaced. Suppose that we have organised an
army of 100,000, of 500,000, men, suppose all those men
obey one head, and suppose (it takes some supposing) we
have a head to lead all those men. That military mass meets
the onset of the enemy, coming from the north; and as it is
three or four times inferior in numbers, we see to our sorrow
that, by virtue of the principles of the modern art of war, it
is defeated and crushed, like the French at Sedan. What is
then to be done? Are the enemy to be allowed to disperse
the remnants of our defeated army, to besiege and capture
Madrid, if they think fit? Is a treaty then to be signed by
which we are bled and mutilated, and are we to remain
satisfied because we are told that our defeat is in accordance
with the precepts laid down by modern civilisation? If warfare were nothing more than a scientific struggle between two
heads playing with masses of men as capital is played with
at the Stock Exchange, it would suffice to take the census into
account for the less to humble themselves before the greater,
for a nation of fifteen million inhabitants to consider itself
virtually defeated by another of twenty or thirty millions.
Faced by the idea of this brutal, though in appearance
civilised, slavery, every noble, independent soul revolts and
seeks a remedy in individual action, standing on the defensive
in accordance with other tactics which equalise the unequal
forces. Military art itself comes to the assistance of this
impulse, and as well as giving rules for the handling of large
masses, also gives rules for the destruction of those same
masses.

We see, then, how an idea that appears as vague and
intangible as that of the territorial spirit bears within itself
the solution of great problems. We feel we ought to have
armies like those of the Continent, and our character asks
for, demands, a peninsular army. The continental soldier
understands solidarity, he feels more courageous when he
knows that along with him, facing the enemy, are one or
two millions of comrades in arms. The peninsular soldier
shrinks up and feels as it were stifled when he finds himself
a cipher in a great mass of troops, because he suspects that

he is not going to act as a human being, but as a machine. Numbers give strength to the one, and take it from the other. Contrariwise, if disaster overtakes any of those great European armies, demoralisation almost immediately sets in, because the main strength lay not in the soldiers, but in the cohesion now broken; in the confidence now lost. The Spanish army is reborn time and again like the phœnix, because its constituent strength is the spirit of the soldier, and that spirit costs nothing, it is a free gift of the soil.

Wherever we turn our steps over the highways of Spain, there comes out to meet us the eternal Sphinx, with her eternal, carping question: is it better to go on living as hitherto—yesterday covered with glory, to-day in the depths of adversity, to-morrow once again raised to prosperity, always organised gipsy-fashion, or are we to break definitely with our bad tradition, and transform ourselves into a well-ordered, well-balanced "modern" nation? Neither the one nor the other. We must not fold our arms and allow what is good in us to become a matter for contempt and scorn; an organisation we must have, but for this to be more than a mere artifice, for it to take firm root among us, it must be in harmony with our national temperament. Though it may seem strange at first sight, such an organisation is quite possible; so much is it within our grasp, that it requires no great effort of imagination, no prolonged meditation, no complicated reasoning. The logical thing stands before our eyes, and if we do not see it, this is because we are distracted by our search for fantastic solutions.

To organise an army which will serve both for war in modern fashion, and a war in Spanish fashion, may seem a titanic task. And yet that task was carried out in the period of our greatest military power. To revive it, it is enough to form small fighting units, so strongly knit as to serve when grouped together as a regular army, and when separated, after a reverse, as centres of stern resistance. A Spanish army cannot neglect the individual warrior spirit of the inhabitants of its soil, it must take it into account, and in extremity rely upon it; its fighting units must not be mere technical organisms, but small-scale reductions of the nation as a whole. We must leave aside artificial organisations,

imitated from the conquerors of to-day or yesterday, and
hold on to what our own needs demand, heedless of what
others are doing. Imitation of the outsider must be limited
to details, all that which is an effective improvement and at
the same time in harmony with our ideas. For it happens
that what in another country is a matter of the first order
is for us of less than second or third; and that what is there
useful is with us useless and harmful, because not in
accordance with what is essential to our organisation.

In a continental army, what is most important is the
mobilisation of great masses, with mathematical and
mechanical precision; secondary to that is the functioning of
the separate units. In a Spanish army, mobilisation, important though it is, is secondary, and the main thing is the
working of the separate companies, which for this reason
should be a reflection, a compendium of the whole country,
of all social classes, of the modern and the traditional, of all
that the nation was and is and wishes to be. The best Spanish
army will be not the one which can count on masses of
soldiers, submissive to a single head, but the one composed
of companies, moving as one man, and having, like the god
Janus, two faces; one turned towards the open plains where
pitched battles are fought, the other towards the mountains
where they will find a final and secure refuge for the defence
of national independence.

*　　　*　　　*

Rare is the book in which no use is made of the ship-
allegory as a symbol of human affairs. There seems no
escape from the well-worn commonplace, for the ideas that
flood our mind when we see a vessel moving over the waters
are those that most clearly reveal to us our universal,
harmonious concept of existence. I myself live in a house
near the sea, surrounded by trees. At times, on the far
horizon, I see the vague outline of a ship rising between sea
and sky, like a bearer of spiritual tidings. Soon I begin to
distinguish the sails and masts, then the hull and some
confused objects in movement, nearer still the crew at their
work; till at last I see the ship enter harbour, warp alongside

and begin to discharge from her hatchway the varied cargo stowed away in her immense maw. And I think that ideas come to us much in the same way, beginning as a divine spark which, taking shape in reality, gradually loses its pristine purity till it sinks, befouled with slime, into the grossest of fleshly forms. For the one fleeting moment when the soul takes delight in the contemplation of an idea which rises pure and spotless from the foam of thought, what anguish afterwards to make that idea sensible in some one of the miserable, weakly forms our scanty powers have at their command; what grief when we see it finally transformed into something material, stained with the impurity from which nothing material is free.

If we may say this of all ideas, with the greatest of exactness can it be applied to the idea of justice; there is none that seems to descend from such heights, none which seems to fall so low, not one which first comes before our eyes so simple and so pure, not one which assumes forms more gross, and more inhuman.

The juridical spirit of a country can be determined by noting on what point in the evolution of the idea of justice its attention has been preferentially fixed. Codes of law are of little worth, they have only an objective value; they must be interpreted by man. It is not enough to say that Spain was ruled first by Roman laws, then by Roman and Germanic laws, and finally by an amalgam of these and of the principles gradually introduced by progress into the ancient legislation. For if we look close at things we find that there has existed and still exists, above this farrago of actual laws, a higher ideal law, the constant law of juridical interpretation, which in Spain has been rather a work of juridical dissolution.

Spain has never had laws of her own; they have been imposed on her by foreign domination; they are products of force. Thus, when during the Reconquest juridical bonds were relaxed, not only did legislative uniformity disappear, we might almost say law itself disappeared, for the charters with which it was thought to find a substitute systematically implied the negation of law. The charter is based on the desire to diversify law in order to adjust it to small social groups; but when this diversity is carried to excess, as it was in many instances, the result may be a legislative atomism so exaggerated that each family wishes to have a code for its own private use. In the Middle Ages our regional States wanted kings of their own, not for their better government, but in order to destroy royal power. Our towns wanted charters which would exempt from the already diminishing authority of these kings, and all social classes wanted privileges by the score. It was then that our country was within an ace of realising its true juridical ideal: that every Spaniard should carry in his pocket a personal charter with a single article, drawn up in these brief, clear, concise terms: "This Spaniard is hereby authorised to do what he jolly well likes."

The practical criterion in juridical matters conforms to positive legislation, and accepts willingly the mutilation of the idea of pure justice involved in its being embodied in institutions and laws. The idealistic criterion is in continuous reaction against the forms of law imposed by necessity and attempts to cling to the rigorous application of what it considers to be justice. The first of these criteria leads to the juridical ideal of society, the uniform, regular, methodical application of laws; the second leads to the juridical ideal of the Christian man: that is, to be guided by justice, not by law, and afterwards to temper the rigours of justice by charity, by pardon generously granted.

In law, as in philosophy, there have been brilliant rhapsodists who have converted pagan into Christian law by dint of very skilful patching, but retaining as the invariable foundation the Roman idea of force, in contrast with the Christian idea of love. It grieves one to say it, but say it one must for it is the truth: after nineteen centuries of evangelisation, the Christian idea has not ruled in the world for a single day. The Gospel has triumphed over hearts and minds; it has not availed to triumph over social instincts, brutally enchained to juridical principles which all our feelings condemn, but which we think adapted for the maintenance of social order, or to put it plainer, for the secure enjoyment of our lives and property.

There is therefore an ineradicable contradiction between

the letter and the spirit of codes, and hence there are countries where little love is felt for the law, and one of these countries is Spain. The anomalies of our character in juridical matters are such that at times they allow the superficial observer to suppose that we are a nation in which all forms of injustice, immorality, abuse and insubordination have their natural abode. There is no people whose literature offers such a copious satirical production directed towards the discrediting of the administrators of the law, in which the courts are looked at more askance, in which less assistance is given to the action of justice. Assistance given! It would be truer to say that when possible the action of justice is hindered, baffled. It is something too deep for us to root out; I have studied law, and I have never been able to bring myself to practise, because I have never been able to look at the mechanism of the law in its serious, noble aspect. This happens to many in Spain, to all those who, like myself, in the midst of mental work never entirely neglect physical labour, never lose contact with the workman and the peasant. As long as a Spaniard is in touch with the prole-tarian classes, who are the archives and the depository of the inexplicable, deep-rooted feelings of a country, he cannot be a man-of-law with the gravity and seriousness which the nature of the charge demands.

One day a peasant came up to me and said: "You are a lawyer; will you tell me what is the penalty for a man who has done such and such a thing in such and such a way? I have been summoned as a witness, and I don't want to act blindly without knowing if I am doing right or wrong." That man is your true Spanish witness, who testifies not what he knows, but what, on previous instruction, he understands will lead to the imposition of the penalty which he believes just. It is not that he distrusts the impartial, intelligent interpretation of the judges, or that these are less upright than those of other countries where different methods obtain; it is simply that he will not abdicate his judgment to that of others. His revolt against the law does not arise from a corruption of his juridical sense; but, on the contrary, from its exaltation. And this exaltation adopts two contrasted forms, which possibly issue in a middle term of justice superior to that which holds where the written law is strictly applied.

The first of these forms is the aspiration towards true justice; casuistry is not welcomed, and exceptions infuriate. What is desired is a short precept, clear as crystal, which admits of no doubt, lends itself to no misconstruction or subterfuge, which is rigorous and, if need be, implacable. When a man reaches a position of prominence and becomes a mark for social criticism, he must be impeccable, incorruptible, perfect, even saintly, and still this juridical quixotism will find some place in which to sink its teeth and wound. How many things that in Spain are stones of stumbling and which proclaimed aloud lower our prestige have I not seen regularly practised in other countries of more accommodating morals?

The second form taken is the excess of compassion, which makes as great an effort to save the fallen as was made to cast him down. For this reason, there is no room in Spain for reformers, that is, people who take on themselves the duty of the repression of immorality, the correction of abuses, the "regeneration of the country". Public opinion follows them till they reach the culminating point—the discovery of the immorality; once this is reached, there follows immediately (not, as may be thought, from slackness of purpose or inconstancy) a right-about movement, and the side of the accused is taken. In this way, unless the paladins of righteousness stop in time and refrain from carrying their work to its logical conclusion, they find themselves opposed by the very same spirit which before gave them encouragement.

This dualism, which, under an appearance of juridical disorder reproved by the commonplace mind, hides the noblest, loftiest idea conceived and practised in the realm of human justice, is a creation of Christian sentiment and Senecan philosophy, where they meet in harmony. As we have seen, the Stoicism of Seneca is not harsh and rigid, it is human and compassionate. Seneca promulgates the law of moral virtue as a goal towards which we all should strive; but he is tolerant with the law-breakers. He demands purity of thought and right intention in will, but he does not fail to recognise, for he himself fell frequently, that the weakness of our nature does not allow us to live in a fixed state of virtue, that there are bound to be backsliders, and that the most a man can do is to bear himself as a man even in the midst of his weaknesses.

The mind that has penetrated most deeply into the soul of our nation, Cervantes, realised so keenly this anomaly in our temperament, that in his immortal book he marks the absolute separation of Spanish justice from the everyday justice of codes and courts of law, the first being incarnated in Don Quixote, the second in Sancho Panza. The only judicial decisions in the book which are moderate, prudent, balanced, are those given by Sancho during his governor-ship of the island. On the other hand, those of Don Quixote are, to all appearance, absurd, for the very reason that they are based on transcendental justice. His excesses reach now towards one extreme, now towards another. All his adven-tures are directed towards upholding ideal justice in the world, and as soon as he comes up with the band of galley-slaves and realises that they are actual criminals, he hastens to set them at liberty. The reasons he gives for releasing these men condemned to the galleys are a compendium of those which animate the revolt of the Spanish spirit against positive justice. One must indeed strive for the rule of justice in this world; but there is no strict right to punish one criminal while others escape through the crevices of the law. After all, general impunity is in conformity with noble and generous aspirations, though they be contrary to the ordered life of society, whereas the punishment of some and the impunity of others are a mockery both of the principles of justice and the feelings of humanity.

It must not be thought that these are ideas which float in the social atmosphere, without any influence on the adminis-tration of justice. However upright the judges may be, however definite the codes, it is impossible for a judge to isolate himself completely from the society in which he lives, and to prevent the infiltration into the precept of the law of the spirit of the people to whom the law is applied. This spirit, working silently, invisibly, but inevitably, ends by destroying the sense in which the laws were originally intended; proceeding with such caution that, without changing a comma of the legal texts, it forces them to say, on occasion, the very opposite of what they had previously said.

The punishment of criminals in Spain is in appearance regulated by a code of law, in reality by this code and the systematic use of reprieve. In another country an attempt would be made to modify the code and bring it into line with gentler, more moderate principles. In Spain we prefer to maintain the rigidity of the code and then to nullify its effects by means of pardon. In other words, we have an anomalous system, in harmony with our anomalous character. We punish in all solemnity and rigour in order to satisfy our desire for justice, and then, without clamour or disturbance, we reprieve the condemned in order to satisfy our desire for clemency.

If this were the place to analyse in detail the facts of our history, it would be seen that many of these owe their origin to our independent juridical spirit, and that very few derive from the ordered action of our regular institutions. A critical, culminating moment in the history of Spain presents itself when Castile, enclosed in the centre of the peninsula, and anxious to terminate the Reconquest and set on foot national unity, begins to hesitate, so to say, inclining now towards Aragon, now towards Portugal. For unity could not be arrived at all at once, inasmuch as the interests and aspirations of the eastern and western kingdoms were, or appeared to be, antagonistic. Furthermore, union was to be brought about by matrimonial alliances, for neither the practice of the time, nor, what is of more importance, the national spirit, encouraged the use of violent means. It was possible for Castile to be either Mediterranean or Atlantic, and both solutions would initiate new historical epochs. It is difficult to speculate, now that we know the consequences of union with the eastern State, whether a union with the western State would have been more fruitful. Nevertheless, the policy of Castile, after the end of the Reconquest, being analogous, not to say identical, with the policy of Portugal, such a union, such an exclusiveness of action, would have produced great effects, possibly less brilliant, but firmer and

E—8

more durable than the continental policy. What is certain is that to the solution to be adopted was linked up the course of historical events in our country and throughout the world, and that by a rare coincidence this problem was presented in purely juridical terms.

On the one side Portugal supported Juana la Beltraneja, and on the other Aragon supported Isabel, and the decision lay with the people of Castile. A people respectful of the written law would not have hesitated, but would have taken sides with Juana, who was in possession of a legal status. Instead of entering on indiscreet investigations as to the relations between the queen and her favourite, the right thing was to stand by juridical principles, universal in matters of legitimacy, without which there can be no constituted family life. What would happen to society if public opinion had the power of changing the entries in the civil register and applying with strict justice the legal maxim—"to every one his own"? The 109th article of our actual Civil Code says: "The child will be presumed legitimate even if the mother has declared its illegitimacy or has been found guilty of adultery." And this precept is no modern invention, it is found in the *Partidas*. But the Castilian people decided to be ruled not by legal precept, but by facts more or less established. When the question of legitimacy was at issue, it wished to penetrate as far as possible into the private apartments of its rulers. And in the case of the unfortunate princess Juana of Castile it was not content with murmurings and insults, which at any rate were understandable; it resorted to the natural law, and relying on it leaped the barriers of the legal code existing at the time and upheld the rights of Isabel. And thus arose the modern nation of Spain.

The spirit of a nation finds its synthesis in its art. We might say that the territorial spirit is the spinal cord, the warlike spirit the heart, the juridical spirit the muscles, and the artistic spirit a kind of network of nerves that links up, unifies and directs all. It is customary to think that religion is superior to art and art superior to science, taking into consideration only the loftiness of the object towards which they tend, but from the standpoint I am adopting, considering them as constituent forces of the soul of the country, the superiority depends on the character of each country. In essence, science, art and religion are one and the same thing; science interprets reality by means of formulas, art by means of images and religion by means of symbols, and it is a rare human activity in which an unmixed interpretation is found. Science makes use of hypotheses, which are nothing more than images utilised to fill up the gaps that cannot be filled by formulas. Art tends to symbolism, and in some cases is transformed into religion (and in periods of decadence into a science which is arbitrary, fantastic, capricious and merely documental). Religion necessarily makes use of art and science in order to humanise its symbols. The real difference lies in the subject; according to the spiritual aptitude predominant in each individual, the world is manifested in one or other form, and all, under different aspects and with varying energy, produce the same 'useful" result, the dignifying of man.

For a mathematician, Newton's binomial theorem is both a work of art and a dogma. An artist will see in it, if he arrives at understanding it at all, an equality of terms which, being apparently dissimilar, contain equivalent quantities, neither more nor less than equality itself: $3+3=5+1$. The mathematician will see in it a complete evolution of ideas, which leads by gradual, intelligible formulas from the hidden to the evident, and a symbol of general value to arrive at a knowledge of new and unknown laws of abstract reality. On the other hand, if a mathematician analyses a love-drama, such as *Los Amantes de Teruel*, he may possibly reduce it to the formula: "infinity=zero", or to a love-equation in which the unknown quantity is the sense of duty. Whereas for an artist the drama will consist in the interior struggle of feelings and in the visible, plastic forms in which these are exteriorised. For the believer the drama will be a kind of religious symbol, and the lovers not blind forces urged by instinct, as in Schopenhauer's idea, but two souls, masters of their fate, ennobled by the abnegation and the dignity with which they transform a human passion opposed to duty into a spiritual, mystic love by means of their death through grief; a transfiguration, a passing from life to a world where duty does not exist, or rather where there is only one duty, that of love; not so much a duty as the delight and joy of spirits.

There are, then, many ways of serving the ideal, and we should only ask of each individual that he serve it in accordance with his native understanding, and of each people that it understand it in accordance with its native genius. Though the expression be a prosaic one, we must use it for its exactness: there is and should be in the case of the ideal a prudent "division of labour". The Jews were a religious people, the Greek artists, the Romans law-givers. All European nations, and those civilised by European influences, are built up on these three foundation stones: the Christian religion, Greek art, Roman law. And though it might appear that by reason of this common origin there should be no nation with one outstanding form of ideal which annuls the others, yet such nations do exist, though we may not in actual fact distinguish them by reason of our nearness to them. The life of a nation always presents an appearance of integrity of functions, because it is not possible to exist without the assistance of all of them, but as time advances it is gradually seen that all these functions are directed by a dominant central force, in which the ideal of each nation may be said to be lodged, and it is then that we begin to distinguish the character of nations and the part played by them with most perfection in history, the drama of mankind.

If we consider their origin, our ideas are the same as those of the other peoples of Europe, who with more or less right have been sharers in the heritage handed down by antiquity. But the combination which we have made of those ideas is exclusively our own, and is different from that made by others, because our race and our climate are different. Quite evident is our inattention to the applied sciences; there is no means of making them take root in Spain, not even by converting scientists into paid servants of the State. Not that there are no scientists, there have been and there are, but when not of mediocre intelligence, they feel themselves drawn to those heights where science loses its special character and combines, now with religion, now with art. Castelar aspires to be an historian, and his studies turn into epico-oratorical poems. Echegaray, mathematician and dramatist, handles numbers with the mastery and deep spiritualism of the Pythagoreans, and in our days Leta-mendi writes on medicine like a Hippocratic philosopher.

Our spirit is religious and artistic, and the religion is often confused with the art. In its turn, the essence of our art is religion in its deepest aspect—mysticism, in alliance with our other characteristic qualities: courage, passion, chivalry. But when we say this, which is what is generally said or thought, we are saying nothing or next to nothing, because much more important than the ideal tendency of an art is the conception and execution of the work, "the work in itself". Nations have personality, style, manner, as artists have; two painters, devotees of the Virgin, paint two Madonnas which are nowise related, and two nations, religious, noble, passionate, may give birth to two opposed styles of art, the reason for the difference being the interesting fact that, whereas the basis of their art lies in the ideals that constitute the race, the technique arises from what I have called the territorial spirit.

Some time since I wrote that Goya was an ignorant genius, and I wrote it with fear and trembling, because I realised that this opinion, for me true then and now, would seem nonsensical or paradoxical to the ordinary way of examining and understanding art matters. Similarly, I believe that Velázquez, who is not only a genius, but the greatest pictoric genius ever known, was as ignorant as Goya. It is not that I find absent the "rules" we hear so much of, nor do I mean the ordinary ignorance which gives rise to anachronisms, falsity in characterisation, wrong interpretation of historical events, the anatomical monstrosities and other defects which injure the total effect of a painting. What I see in them is the lack of technical thought, or to put it more plainly, that the artist does not know when his work has arrived at its true point of execution, because he allows himself to be guided only by the impulse of his genius. And as genius is a most uncertain faculty, it is rare that the hand guided by it brings a work to a proper finish;

at any moment during the execution the work *is being done*, but in one only it *is done*; and the hand often stops by mere caprice, not at the point of supreme perfection. This insecurity produces, in the inspired moments of great geniuses, those original creations which form an epoch in the history of art; but, accepted as a systematic procedure, it is the cause why mediocre minds, and at times even great ones, fail so disgracefully; the cause, also, why those same original creations do not, as they ought, bring about an ennoblement of art in the countries in which they appear, but rather contribute to the formation of bad taste, and hasten the decadence and the destruction of the ideal.

The characteristic indicated is not to be taken as exclusive to Velázquez or Goya; it is constant and universal in our country, for it springs spontaneous from our love of independence. Hence, in Spain, there are no middle terms. The small artists, as well as the great, go on the principle of "seeing how it will turn out". When they begin to work they generally have only a vague notion of what they are going to produce and an absolute confidence in their own forces, in their innate genius, unless indeed, as in the ballads sung by blind men in the streets, they simply "trust in God and in the Queen of Heaven". Whenever your genuine Spaniard takes up his pen or his brush or any other instrument of artistic production, you may conclude, without the slightest fear of mistake, that that man is equally capable of creating a masterpiece or of giving birth to some stupendous monstrosity.

There exists nothing in Spanish art superior to Don Quixote, and Don Quixote was not only created after the Spanish manner, but is our most typical work, for Cervantes was not content with being an "independent", he was a *conquistador*, the greatest of them all. The others conquered lands for Spain; he, shut up in a prison, conquered Spain itself. When Cervantes begins to conceive his work, he carries within himself a portentous genius; outside of him there are only figures that move as divine intuitions. He collects these figures and one might say drives them forward as a muleteer does his animals, encouraging them with uncouth terms of affection, mingled with impartial and opportune blows. Do not look for any deeper artifice in the Quixote. It is written in prose, and it is like that rare mystic poetry in which it is indifferent whether we start at the beginning or the end, for every verse is a pure, independent sensation, like a Platonic idea.

How are we to explain that Lope de Vega, with his original and fertile dramatic genius, has not left us a "finished" work such as *Hamlet*? It is not that the creative faculty in Lope was less than in Shakespeare, but that Shakespeare fired after taking good aim and almost always hit the mark, whereas Lope hardly ever hit the mark because he fired into the air. This difference is so evident that in Spain itself Lope has been relegated to a second place, after Calderón. Calderón made use of theatrical types without the exuberance and spontaneity of those of Lope, but he knew how to concentrate his attention better, and to inspire into his characters and scenes a certain interior intensity and emotion, without which no work can be lasting. Not that Calderón professed more fixed esthetic principles than Lope; when artistic independence is so exaggerated as it is in our country, principles are of little avail, for everyone does what best pleases him; the failures and the successes depend largely on chance, on a happy intuition interpreted with more or less good fortune. To pass the time during vacation, a student from Salamanca starts to write *La Celestina*, and wins for himself front rank in Spanish literature.

If the Spanish theatre sinks from the heights of Lope to the abysmal depths in which dwelt the sorry crew which served Moratín for the writing of his *Comedia Nueva*, the blame is not to be imputed to the followers of Don Hermógenes, but to Lope, or more than to Lope, to our national character. The lowest attempt to be artists as well as the highest; they will not stop at a respectable medium form of art, they fling themselves into the depths of artistic savagery. I once saw in Seville an *Immaculate Conception*, a typical Sevillian commercial product, and it made me say to myself: "The author of this atrocity is a mere house-painter, but one must be just and admit that he wields his brushes with the same skill with which Murillo must have used his 'pencils'."

I do not accept the narrow, mean, more French than Spanish criterion of Moratín, who was well acquainted with our art, but never succeeded in understanding it. If there is no human remedy for our artistic failings, it is better that we be alternatively geniuses and idiots than that we be constantly correct and mediocre. But this must not prevent us pointing out that our characteristic, as regards artistic technique, is an exalted love of independence, which leads us to pay no attention to anything, at best to proceed through a spirit of opposition and finally to give no heed even to ourselves, to work without reflection and to expose ourselves to the greatest failures.

When the French theatre of Corneille held sway in Germany, there arose a dramatic critic of extraordinary insight and intelligence, Lessing, who waged war on it in the name of the very principles of the classic theatre, of which the French was a false interpretation, and upheld the superiority of the Romantic theatre of the Spaniards and the English. And, nevertheless, the theatre of Corneille was also a sort of reflection of the Spanish theatre; it was a monstrous mixture of the sobriety and severity of the Grecian stage with the dramatic intrigues and artifices invented by the fertile fantasy of Lope de Vega. I quote this example to show how dangerous our art is to those who try to imitate it. The author of the "Dramaturgy" himself, enamoured though he was of the poetry, vivacity and naturalness of our theatre, made great reservations in respect to theatrical artifices invented without thought or discretion. Consequently our influence in the development of the German stage was a secondary one, and Schiller was able to say later on, with good show of reason, that "the Germans had had for guides only the Greeks and Shakespeare".

The most interesting point about these anomalies which arise from our character is that there is no means of avoiding them by the imitation of good models and the formation of artistic schools. We do not want to imitate, but even if we did we could not do it fruitfully; for our models, by reason of their excessive personal force, are not imitable. This explains the anomalous fact that, for all our independence, our art, like our history, is one continued invasion of foreign influences. Once left to ourselves we destroy our own art, and to restore it we must go outside Spain in order to strike a balance of taste. Hardly has this been somewhat refined, when we go back to our old ways. Study the history of Spanish art in the nineteenth century, the history of the art which comes out into the open (for there is an art such as music, which in its genuine, elevated Spanish style has hardly emerged from the churches), and the proof of what I have just said will be found. We have had two groups of painters which have attempted, one in France and the other in Italy, to find some way of restoring our art; and hardly has the artistic level of the nation been raised a little, when the Spaniards, the independents, appear, and with them the first signs of insubordination and disorder. As always, we shall have great works created by the masters, and a rapid decadence provoked by the daring and the recklessness of the apprentices.

As regards poetry and the novel, it is clear to everyone that we have had, or have, representatives of all the artistic tendencies of Europe, without ever succeeding in forming groups, on account of our tendency to devirtualise the conventional forms, however great acceptation they may have found, in order to convert them into a private, personal style. It is equally clear that no poet, or novelist, or mere writer will accept lessons from those recognised and honoured as masters; all want to be heads, whether of mouse or of lion matters not, and instead of forming an Army of Letters we are nothing but a guerrilla band of literary men.

Is it absolutely impossible to modify these instincts of insubordination which are destroying, annihilating us? I do not think so. In spite of our spirit of independence, we have succeeded in setting up two nations in the peninsula; not one, it is true, but at any rate not more than two; consequently, from this point of view, some cohesion has been given to the territorial spirit. On the other hand, in the arts, instead of advancing, we are receding. By an inexplicable error, it has been believed that the anarchy originates in regional literatures, whereas these are, on the contrary, forces making for discipline. By another error of still greater magnitude, it has been thought that centralisation would bring cohesion, when what it really does is to withdraw individuals from those places where they would undergo the beneficial influence of a moderate intellectual atmosphere in order to launch them into the vacuum and the solitude of a milieu more cultured, no doubt, but more restless and incoherent, in which they will find nothing to serve them as a support, nothing to repress their natural tendency towards exaggeration and lack of balance. Spain, as a nation, has not yet been able to create such a general, regulating atmosphere, because its greatest energies have been wasted in heroic enterprises. Hardly is the nation set on foot when our spirit leaves the course marked out for it and spreads over the whole world in search of external, empty glory; and the country is converted into a reserve garrison, a pensioners' hospital, a breeding-ground for beggars. What wonder, then, that in such a rarefied atmosphere the few men of worth who were left should feel the urge to give free rein to their faculties without understanding whither they were going or where they ought to stop? Reflection is not, as is thought, a purely internal act; it is rather a work of unification of the thoughts inspired in us by the reality in which we live, and even the most independent spirits can be made to submit to work for a common cause if they are surrounded by other minds capable of restraining and imprisoning them.

We possess a *History of Esthetic Ideas in Spain*, by Menéndez y Pelayo, but we do not (I was going to say "cannot") possess a history of our technical processes, of our styles, of our schools; because in Spain it is not easy to bring them into relation with a higher unity, a general concept, a true school. Consequently, the high points of our art are not represented by groups united by community of doctrine, but by dispersed geniuses who, like Cervantes or Velázquez, form a school to themselves. In France there are four or five thousand journalists, who without an idea in their heads write with all the aplomb of literary giants. The patriotic spirit forces them to form nuclei, and around each sun there revolve innumerable planets, satellites, asteroids and even bolides. It is true that this petty race does nothing of great profit, but neither does it do much harm; whereas in Spain it only serves to level down the esthetic feeling of the nation.

As has been said by my friend Navarro y Ledesma, one of the few Spaniards who still think in Spanish, the French language is like an overcoat and the Spanish like a cloak. There is no more individualistic article of attire than the Spanish cloak, none more difficult to wear, especially when made of heavy material and reaching to the feet. No doubt about it, the Spanish language is a cloak and the majority of Spanish writers wear it dragging on the ground.

Incalculable is the number of men of genius lost to Spanish art by the wars and colonisations; and the loss was a double one, for there was lost all that which they failed to create and the influence they might have had on those who were left. This idea is no product of empty sentimentalism. I find no great difference between life and death, for I believe that what really lives are ideas. But the individual must also live, as being the creator of ideas, and the species, as being necessary for the preservation of those ideas. I do not then attach much importance to death, still less to the form in which it overtakes us; what does afflict me is the thought that in the dead body are left the present or future creations of the spirit. There are many ways of loving one's country, and it is right that each should love it after the fashion which is most natural to him and will most contribute to its prestige. We have to such an extreme lost all sense of perspective, that we give importance only to the shedding of blood. Those who do not fight with arms or at least with eloquent speeches are the mere "dead wood" of society, are regarded with contempt. Long since, Goethe said in this connection: "I have tried to reach the highest point within my grasp in those matters to which I felt drawn by nature; I have toiled with passion, I have neglected no means, no effort in the realisation of my work; if anyone has done as much as I, let him raise his hand." Nothing could be said with more nobility and justice. The Hottentot, the Matabele and the Zulu also shed their blood in defence of their native land; amongst cultivated peoples that is not enough. One must struggle for the idealistic aggrandisement of the great family from which one has sprung, and this aggrandisement demands something more than the mere sacrifice of life.

The Golden Age of the Spanish Arts, admirable as it was,

is a mere hint of what it might have been if, when the Reconquest had ended, we had concentrated our forces and had applied them to give form to our own ideals. The energy accumulated in the struggle against the Moors was not only warlike energy, as many believe; it was also, as we shall see, energy of the spirit. If historic destiny had not set us on the slope which it actually did, just as our national energy was transformed into action beyond our borders, it might have been maintained within the limits of our territory, in a life more intimate, more intense, and have made of our nation a Christian Greece.

§ B

THE lines of the external policy of Spain in the Modern Age might be graphically represented by the compass-card. The policy of Castile was African or southern, for the fall of Granada and the end of the Reconquest could not be the final blow directed against the Moors. The Moslem power was still vigorous and a new attack was to be feared, for Mahometanism bears within itself a germ of violence which to-day seems extinguished and to-morrow reappears incarnate in a new race which gives it fresh vigour and life. Apart from this, it was logical that the repulse should follow the lines of the aggression; that it should not end on our own territory, but should be carried into that of our invaders. The policy of Aragon was Mediterranean and eastern, and as when Aragon and Castile united, they did so on equal terms, forming not so much a union as a mutual-aid society, in the same way that Aragon helped in the Conquest of Granada, Castile was to help Aragon in its Italian enterprises. Again, by the chance of history, in that same camp of Santa Fe, where the military nucleus was formed which afterwards passed to the battlefields of Italy, there was born the idea of accepting the plans of Columbus, and therewith the initiation of our American or western policy. We had, then, three of the cardinal points; only one was lacking, the north, and this came opportunely when the Low Countries were incorporated with Spain. From the conjunction of these contrasted policies arose all kinds of secondary ones, and soon there was no European nation with which, on one pretext or another, we had not to settle matters either by diplomacy or by war.

The extreme positivist point of view which inspires historical studies to-day obliges historians to set out all facts on the same plane and to take supreme pride in exactitude and impartiality. Instead of historical pictures, we are given skilfully drawn-up summaries of records, and impartiality is secured by the very simple method of never saying what the facts signify. And yet the essential thing in history is the linking up of the facts with the spirit of the country where they occurred; only at this price can a true, logical, useful history be written. What fruits can be obtained from a series of events exactly stated and based on trustworthy proofs, if equal value is given to them all, if they are portrayed in the same relief, if there is no indication as to which are in accordance with the character of the nation and which opposed to it, which are favourable and which contrary to the natural evolution of each territory, considered, together with its inhabitants, as an historic personality?

Those who write histories of Spain fix their attention specially on the Modern Period, because it is nearer to them, and they see it in the foreground as the principal subject of the picture they propose to paint. The notion is a wrong one, it is bad perspective. In history it is not possible to place one set of facts before others like figures or objects in a picture. Everything is fused into the personality of the nation; and it is from this viewpoint that the relative importance of historical events must be estimated. When several centuries have passed and another modern epoch arrives, the one we to-day call modern will no longer be so. Its name will have to be changed, and it will be seen that it is not only a question of changing a name, but of changing also the total significance of the events which filled the period. The modern history of to-day's viewpoint will then be seen as an anomalous phase of our general history.

We have had, after certain periods lacking unity of character, a Hispano-Roman period, a Hispano-Visigoth period and a Hispano-Moorish period. The succeeding ones were Hispano-European and Hispano-American, an epoch of formation the former, of expansion the latter. What we have never had is a purely Spanish period, in which our spirit, once constituted, should give its fruits on its own soil; and as we have not had such a period, the logic of history demands that we should have one, and that we should bestir

ourselves to be its initiators. The action of a nation through
the medium of force is an important one; more important
is its action in the realm of ideas, and this reaches its highest
point when external activities are abandoned and the
national vitality concentrated within its own territory.

At the beginning of the Modern Age there were in Spain
two political tendencies, those of Castile and Aragon, the
African and the Italian. After the union of Castile and
Aragon the second policy should have lost some ground.
The exploration and conquest of America, which opened
such a breach in our national life, had also its justification in
our character, in our faith, in the providential destiny which
fell so heavily on our shoulders. But our action in the centre
of Europe was a policy of immeasurable absurdity, an
illogicality whose only excuse was and is the fact that it was
based on ideas then in vogue in the matter of political theory
and practice. When Spain, a peninsular nation, set about
acting like the continental nations, she condemned herself
to certain ruin. Whereas a country is strengthened by
acquiring new territories within its natural sphere of action,
it is, on the other hand, weakened by the absorption of
those which involve contingencies opposed to its special,
permanent interest. The power of England is upheld by her
not departing from this line of action; it is a power which is
based on the occupation of strategic points, which can be
defended "island-fashion". England might have occupied
the Low Countries at periods when it would not have been
necessary to employ great forces for the occupation; she has
limited herself to bringing about the holding of the territory
opposite her by small, weak nations, so as to be thus free
from exposure to invasion. If she had gone beyond that, a
similar fate to ours would have befallen her. A wrong road
in policy destroys a nation, be it the greatest nation in the
world.

Spain committed this mistake, and when she committed it
there were some who realised, as by a vague instinct, the
perils to which it left us open. Of the many who realised it,
some died and others were executed. To my mind, the death
of Cisneros (opportune for himself, as saving him from
exposure to the blast of foreign air that Charles of Ghent

brought with him) was the death of Castile. And the
execution of the *Comuneros* was the punishment inflicted on
the refractory spirits who were unwilling to tread the new
paths opened up to Spanish policy. The *Comuneros* were
neither "liberals" nor "liberators", as many would have
us think; they were not romantic heroes inflamed by new
and generous ideas, and overthrown in the fight at Villalar
by the numerical superiority of the imperial troops and the
driving rain that lashed their faces and prevented them
seeing the enemy. They were simply rigid, exclusive
Castilians who were upholding the traditional, national
policy against the innovating, European policy of Charles V.
And as far as the battle of Villalar is concerned, it seems
now to be established that it was never even fought.

In the rising of the *Comunidades* of Castile, it happened, as is
nearly always the case, that right was on both sides, and that
the dispute rose about everything but the real cause of the
disorder, possibly because the opposing parties had no exact
idea of their respective claims. In our days the policy of
State-intervention is in vogue; all social classes look to the
State for help, and some of them demand its transformation
into a Purveyor-General of Happiness. Along these lines,
political power will gradually be changed into paternal
authority, and the State will be obliged to seek out new ways
in order to fulfil its brand-new social functions. Then will
rise up the protest of those who have been silent during the
discussion, of those who are surprised at the inevitable
consequences. In the same way, when the Spanish nation
was being constituted, royal authority was exalted above all
others, it was asked to assume the direction of all the constituent forces of the country, rendered insubordinate by the
abuse of privilege, and it was encouraged to strive for
political aggrandisement in accordance with the ideas of
the period; namely, the raising up of strong nationalities.
And as soon as the royal power set itself to the task, there
broke out the rebellion of the prudent men, those who saw
national policy being transmuted into dynastic policy.

Once this initial error is admitted, it must be recognised
that Charles V was the man for the moment. There was no
one in Spain capable of understanding his policy, and this

shows, without need of further proof, that his policy was
foreign to our interests, even though based on incontro-
vertible rights and vague aspirations of our country.
Charles V plays in our history a part analogous, though in
inverse sense, to that played by Napoleon in the history of
France. Napoleon made France an insular nation, Charles V
made Spain a continental nation. He was able to carry
forward the varying, contradictory policies which presented
themselves almost simultaneously; he attended to the Low
Countries, to Italy, to Tunis, to America. He took it all in
with his wide, keen, certain glance, but his work was of the
most personal nature, for he looked at Spain only from outside and attributed to us the same ambition that afflicted
himself, a man of the Continent.

When power passed from Charles V to Philip II, it is at
once seen that the policy of the House of Austria is about to
become a danger to Europe and to be the ruin of our nation.
Philip II was a Spaniard and saw everything through a
Spaniard's eyes, with independence and exclusiveness. He
could, therefore, not be content with the appearance of
power; he wanted the reality. Philip was a man remarkable
for his honesty, he is a mirror in which many monarchs
might gaze who pride themselves on their power over
States the preservation of which causes them to accept
humiliations no less degrading than those suffered by
courtiers to maintain themselves in positions won by
intrigue and favouritism. Philip II wanted to be *de facto*
what he was *de jure*, he wished both to reign and to govern,
he wished the Spanish rule to be no mere label for the
satisfaction of national vanity, but an effective power in
possession of all the faculties and attributes of sovereignty, a
positive force which would impress the well-marked features
of our national character on all the countries submitted to
our action, and by reflection, if possible, throughout the
world. It was from this standpoint that he visualised and
attacked all the political problems that his times presented
to him, and to his tenacity were due both his triumphs and
his failures.

For another nation, the religious conflict that arose on the
appearance of the Reformation in the Low Countries would

have been of relatively easy solution. When the first moments of resistance were passed, and the proportions reached by the heresy realised, a compromise would have been sought which would leave the political domination unimpaired. This would have been done by France, likewise a Catholic country, but less rigorist, more attached to political prestige than to religious ideas, as is proved by her alliances with Protestants, and even with Turks, when it so suited her interests. Spain alone was capable of approaching the problem from the point of view she actually took, and of risking her material rule in order to maintain the authority of religion. And whereas the other nations would have ended by losing their dominion at a later period, leaving no trace of their passage, we lost ours before our time, but we left one more Catholic country in Europe.

The policy of Philip II had the merit of all policy which is straightforward and logical; it served to mark out the dividing lines and to make us realise the seriousness of the enterprise undertaken by Spain when she left the paths laid down by national policy. If Philip II did not win a complete triumph, if he left as an inheritance an inevitable catastrophe, the fault was not his, but of the impossibility of adapting himself and his country to the tactics demanded by a continental policy. A nation cannot impose its authority merely with military and naval forces, it must possess ideas which are flexible and lend themselves to rapid diffusion. These ideas cannot be invented; they spring, as we see constantly in the case of France, from the fusion of ideas introduced from outside with native ideas. The spontaneity of native thought must be sacrificed, and "general ideas" must be worked out, such as will gain currency in all countries, if durable political influence is desired. We, by our very temperament, are unfitted for such manipulations, and our spirit has not succeeded in triumphing except by violence. I believe that, in the long run, it is the most exclusive, most original spirit which imposes itself, but when it succeeds in doing so, it has no longer any political influence; its influence lies in the realm of ideas, as did that of the Greeks over the Romans.

With Philip II there disappears from our nation the

synthetic sense; I mean the power of appreciating in their totality our varied political interests. Spain holds out a long time with the instinct for self-preservation, but without ever even considering which, in case of necessity, is the interest to be sacrificed; rather putting on the same level the passing and fleeting aspects of our policy with the essential and permanent. The fundamental idea of our governors was that political strength depended on extent of territory; as long as this was not reduced the nation preserved entire its prestige and its vitality. So we kept ourselves going, or rather were kept going by our army, a centre of resistance which checked the dismemberment, and which at times came to be the sole representative of the nation, with more right to the title than the immense mass of territories and peoples which formed it.

To my mind, the really sad thing about our decadence is not the decadence itself, but the refinement of stupidity of which repeated proof was given by those placed at the head of public affairs in Spain. At most one finds an occasional man competent to carry out a mission entrusted to him, but we never come across one who sees and judges national policy from a lofty or at, any rate, a central point of view. It happened with all of them as, in popular phrase, happens to old musicians, "they can just keep in time".

It might well have been a benefit for Spain if the long and painful descent, which began with the Peace of Westphalia and ended with the Peace of Utrecht, had been a rapid fall, in which we might probably have saved our national unity. But scattered as our forces were in order to attend to so many points at the one time, weakened by a constant output of energy, which increased the nearer our ruin approached, the bonds which held together the different Spanish regions began to loosen, and the nation was on the point of splitting asunder. It did split in part, for Portugal, whose union with us was most recent, ended by winning her independence.

It is not just to demand of the men of those times the exact knowledge of what our interests were that we to-day possess, judging events at a distance and with different political criteria. But it is just to declare that even with the ideas that then obtained, affairs would have been more wisely handled if our statesmen had been equal to the occasion, or, at least, if they had been capable of separating what was permanent in the nation—the home country, the united peninsula, from what was accidental—the dependent States and the colonies. The confusion at this point was so complete that in one treaty—that óf the Pyrenees—they judged from the same standpoint and defended with equal tenacity the Spanish dominion over Portugal (whose revolt was favoured and supported by France) and the personal interests of the Princes of Condé.   However high a concept of political loyalty may be professed, it is never permissible to sacrifice the interests of a nation, which is something substantive and permanent, to the advantage of a private individual, whose services can be privately recompensed.

The policy of the Bourbons was no better than that of the Habsburgs in this respect.   The notion is still entertained that the greatness of the nation comes from ·outside itself, that its strength is quantitative, lying in extent of territory. This is the system generally followed by the ruined noble- man. ·No question of reducing expenses lest he might reveal (what in reality everyone sees) that the house is crumbling: usurious borrowing, futile displays of power to inspire confidence, marriages in which a providential dowry is the aim, and similar mean ·expedients.   None other was our policy when the House of Bourbon came to the throne.   The matter which made most noise at the time was the famous question of the Duchies, and our political masterpiece the attempt at galvanisation made by the intriguer Alberoni. The Spirit of Spain, vitiated by a régime built on artifice, lacking a strong arm to compel it to seek its salvation in the only direction possible—the restoration of the nation's energies—gratefully accepts all the political panaceas offered it by the jobbers of diplomacy, and for a long period drags its way through the depths of collective beggary, decked in the tinsel of fictitious, ridiculous grandeur.

*   *   *

The Modern Age of our history is not yet closed, for an epoch does not end until new facts arise which mark out a

new direction. In our days the attempts made in the reign of
Charles III have been renewed; it looks for a time as if we
are about to enter the promised land, but soon complications
arise which overthrow the work started and leave us in our
everlasting provisional state.   We are still discussing the
form the government should take and the territorial organisation of the country; discussion going on for ever about everything.   The forces which before were wasted on political
adventures abroad are now wasted in talking at home; we
have passed from deeds to words, but we have not yet passed
from words to that action in internal affairs which is the
final term and natural objective of our political life.   Some
things we have restored afresh, but there is one thing still to
be restored: a common purpose.   When all Spaniards, even
at the sacrifice of theoretical convictions, accept a system of
law fixed, indisputable, and over a long period unchanged,
and set themselves unanimously to labour at the task which
interests us all, then it may be said that we have entered on a
new historic period.

   The starting point for the external policy of a country is
the national policy, for on the latter depends the course to be
set for the former.   Likewise, the starting point for the
internal policy is the idea that is held of the part which the
country ought to play in foreign affairs.   For example: the
internal policy of Prussia, before the constitution of the
German Empire, was subordinated to the idea of setting up
that empire; the external policy of Italy, at the present time,
is subordinated to the requirements of her internal policy,
the need of consolidating Italian unity.   If we decide on
what ought to be in the future the external policy of Spain,
we shall have a basis on which to construct our internal
policy, and once this is accepted we shall find the strength
necessary to satisfy our national aspirations.   Consequently,
to my mind, Spain cannot at present have any sure, fixed
external policy, because she lacks an internal constitution
robust enough to allow her to follow a course in harmony
with her new interests.   For this reason, we have only to
study what these interests are in order to base upon them
our internal political organisation.

   The point where the horizon is clearest is the north.   Our

former fatal Continental policy is absolutely finished, dead and buried. Apart from commercial and neighbourly relations, there is nothing to oblige Spain to interfere in European affairs. We have a natural frontier definitely marked out, and our territorial policy is that of voluntary abstention, which if it were not as logical as it is should be accepted from mere self-respect. When an eminent actor realises that his powers are weakening through the inevitable action of time, there is open to him no other worthy, noble solution than to retire in time. He may not degrade himself by accepting lesser parts, till he sinks to that of first or second servant, whose intervention in the play is limited to pronouncing the ritual phrase, "Dinner is served, my lady". Spain has been the great tragic actor of Europe; she cannot accept as a gracious concession the part of a Great Power, which some restless but ignorant politicians imagine will suffice to give us the strength we no longer have. Our criterion in this matter ought, I believe, to be so strict that we should refuse all intervention in European affairs, even with a view to solving our own gravest political problems. However great the benefits obtained they would never suffice to compensate for the pernicious effects necessarily resultant from political action opposed to what is essential to our territorial situation.

It will no doubt seem daring to assert thus roundly that there is pending for us no problem of Continental politics. Have we not in Spain—I shall be asked—two problems which affect our national unity, and which are European in the sense that their solution partly depends on the politics of Europe? For in Spain it is generally believed that the restoration of Gibraltar and the unification of the peninsula are questions which demand of Spain, by exception, an abandonment of her isolation, whereas the truth is that both of these motives justify and support, even more vigorously, if possible, our systematic isolation.

The restoration of Gibraltar should be a task essentially and exclusively Spanish. It might be a task for Europe, if all the European nations, interested as they are in the freedom of the Mediterranean, judged it opportune to intervene by peaceful methods, as they did in the opening up of the great navigable waterways in the interior of the Continent. But apart from this, Spain cannot seek the support of this or that political group in Europe, in order to obtain a restoration by force, for such help would have to be paid too dearly, and would make our weakness as evident as in the present situation.

There is no humiliation or dishonour in the recognition of the superiority of an adversary: it is abundantly clear that England remains supreme in all the seas of the globe; few countries have escaped from her abuse of power, favoured by disunion on the Continent. Against such abuses the wisest policy is to make oneself strong and to inspire respect. An act of force such as the occupation of Gibraltar has a certain practical utility: it serves as a regulator of the national energies and prevents the reckless from raising their voices too high. Gibraltar is a source of strength for England as long as Spain remains weak; if Spain were strong it would become a weak point for England and lose its *raison d'être*. It may be scientifically laid down that a strong and vigorous nation, however small it may be, runs no risk of being humiliated in its territory; it is only divided, disorganised nations that excite the desire of inflicting such territorial injuries, and it is only against such nations that high political piracy can be engaged in with impunity.

England is not a nation which inspires affection, rather does its strength make it feared or hated; generally when a nation is looked on kindly it is not doing very well. Political sympathies are rather like feelings of compassion or pity in the relations between human beings. But, fortunately, sentiment in political matters is quoted very low at present, and all these questions may be stated in bald, egoistic terms, and there is in this frank egoism a distinct advantage over the cautious, hypocritical egoism of "classic" diplomacy. In accordance with this new criterion, we can, then, say without scandal to political morals, that amongst all the nations of Europe, Spain is, after Italy, the one most interested in England's naval supremacy being maintained for a long time to come. In this aspect we are in the same position as that broken-down gentleman who could not bring himself to get rid of an ancient servitor who was too wasteful.

"It is not affection that makes me keep him," he would say, "but the fear that his successor might reduce me to beggary." And if any one of those who are irritated by the affront implied by Gibraltar think this idea by no means brilliant, let him understand that it was whispered in my ear by the wise Sancho Panza, who was every bit a son of Spain and of La Mancha as was Don Quixote.

Before we clap hands in childish glee at the downfall of one Power, we must consider what Power is going to succeed it. We cannot be the heirs of England, and we must look to see what Power would take up the inheritance in the event of her overthrow. There are a hundred possible solutions, and none as straightforward as the *status quo*, or more favourable. To my mind, the nation most to be feared as a maritime power is England, for the reason that this power is in conformity with her territorial character. No Continental nation can by itself reach the point reached by England, who has two advantages in her favour: first, she has no immediate connection with the Continent, still less with the Mediterranean coasts, and second, she has now reached the maximum of absorption, and finds herself already obliged to resort to defensive measures. Her power, then, would be useful to Europe if, deprived of her aggressive tendency, she could maintain her position as superintendent of public order amongst the nations. On the other hand, a Continental maritime Power, France or Russia, for example, would be a constant cause of perturbation and a menace to the independence of other countries, which might be attacked both by land and sea. England must confine herself to the occupation of isolated points on the coast; a Continental nation would have arms and means to impose her will over the whole extent of a territory.

To find an advantageous substitute for England's maritime supremacy there are two theoretical solutions, which I indicate merely as theories: the neutralisation of the Mediterranean, or a balance of maritime power equivalent to neutralisation. A time must come when European hegemony in the world can no longer be maintained by the actual means and will demand a concentration of forces, and as this hegemony finds its main support in naval power, it will be necessary to set up a nucleus, a centre of conciliation, in the specifically European sea, the Mediterranean. Neither a diplomatic *entente* nor an alliance subscribed to on paper will suffice; there must be a visible, tangible fact, to serve as trustworthy proof of unity of action, and which of its own virtue, without the need of immediate resort to violence, will maintain the supremacy which Europe to-day exercises by means of unstable coalitions. The neutralisation of the Mediterranean would set free large naval forces, thus allowing of an increase in the expansive movement of Europe. The balance of naval power would be a basis of common understanding and action, provided always that all European nations were represented, and especially the weaker ones, who would serve with all the more loyalty and disinterestedness as mediators and maintainers of the peace.

But both these solutions, to develop which would require a volume specially dedicated to these grave matters, are at present devoid of practical value, because the nations have not succeeded in shedding their private ambitions. When plans are laid for destroying the supremacy of England, it is not in order to substitute for it a general power acting in harmony, but to inherit that supremacy, to supplant it by another as exclusive and possibly more dangerous. The two peaceful solutions indicated are like the ace of spades and the ace of clubs in the game of *tresillo*, they are trump cards which Europe keeps in reserve for the day of supreme difficulty, and that day has not yet arrived. For the present, the prudent thing is to support the Power least liable to do harm.

Malta is geographically a dependency of Italy, but this fact does not prevent Italy taking her stand beside England. Spain is not under this obligation, because she has other seas open to her, she is not enclosed within the Mediterranean. She has no need of alliances and should not form them with any stronger nation, for in treaties with the powerful it is the unfavourable clauses which are effective, the advantageous ones being at least problematic. But Spain *is* interested in the maritime supremacy of England being maintained.

Gibraltar is a standing offence, which we have in part deserved by our lack of good government, but it does not hinder the normal development of our country, nor does it afford sufficient reason for our sacrificing other more valuable interests, in order to anticipate somewhat (in the most favourable hypothesis) a fact whose logical realisation is indicated in the course of the restoration of our nationality. It seems absurd, no doubt, that our own interests are linked up with those of the one nation with whom we have genuine grounds for ill-feelings, but in the recognition and acceptance of such anomalies lies at times the highest political wisdom.

The problem of Iberian unity is neither European nor Spanish; as the words themselves indicate, it is peninsular. Though some European countries may be interested in maintaining the division of the peninsula, it does not follow that the question is a European one. If all these countries agreed to our establishing this happy unity, that would give us no reason for committing an aggression, nor, though people may think otherwise, would anyone in Spain be found capable of doing it. On the other hand, if Spain and Portugal voluntarily decided on union, no country in Europe could object to an agreement which in no way affects the political balance of the Continent. Union should be the exclusive work of the parties to the union; it is an internal matter in which resort to external help is dangerous. The example of Italy affords abundant proof of this.

Similarly, I have never understood the question of Iberian unity as a purely Spanish one. The unitary epidemic which still afflicts all the countries of the globe attacks us all with more or less force. There was a time when I too felt saddened at the sight of the map of our peninsula printed in two colours; I shall go further, my sorrow was increased when I saw the division of the peninsula running north and south, cutting through mountains and rivers and forming two incomplete nations. How much more logical would be a division from west to east, leaving to the north a kingdom of Spain, and to the south a kingdom of Andalusia, a Vandal State, half-African, half-European. But I have since noted so many artificial unions that I have changed my opinion. If we had to be united in the fashion of England and Ireland, Sweden and Norway, Austria and Hungary, better for us to continue separate, and that this separation serve at least to create feelings of brotherhood, impossible in a forced régime of union. The union of different nationalities into a single nation can have no other useful human purpose than that of bringing into close contact diverse civilisations, so that from this contact a spiritual renewal may be produced. This is an end which may perhaps be better obtained without the support of material, political domination.

The union of many is easier than the union of two. The enterprise of confederating the German States into a single empire is child's play compared with the problem of Iberian unity, in which, from the fact that the union aimed at is between two, there is no way of hiding appearances, and the greater strength of one must be clearly perceived. Even if the equality were absolute, the weaker party would think itself humiliated, and if motives were lacking would search for pretexts to nourish its suspicions. Hence the idea of some politicians to dissolve the Spanish nation, to revive the former regions and to base unity on some form of confederation. These politicians are like boys playing cards, who when they lose will not agree, but shuffle the cards, saying: "That trick doesn't count"; or like a man who goes bird-snaring, and though he catches a lot in one pull of the net, decides that not one bird shall escape, and sets free those already caught so that they may lure the one that was not; never thinking that in all likelihood not one bird will return within a stone's throw of the nets.

One cannot play tricks with history; events are not repeated to suit our caprice, nor can we turn back to rectify what was at the start badly done. True political science does not consist in such scheming, but in working with perseverance to ensure that the loyal acceptance of actual facts, advancing not receding, may bring us in the future to the solution that seems most logical. This is the one way in which man can intervene with profit in the progress of events; by recognising reality and submitting to it, not by attempting to change it or to burke it. The unity of the Iberian peninsula does not justify new territorial divisions, nor any change in the form of government, because the cause of separation does not lie in anything so accidental, but in something much deeper which we dare not conceal from ourselves. This cause is the historic antipathy between Castile and Portugal, arising possibly from the close similarity of their characters. The only sensible policy, then, is to set ourselves to destroy that lack of understanding and to set up an intellectual and a sentimental unity. To effect this and to prevent Portugal seeking support elsewhere and remaining hostile to us we must bury for ever the well-worn theme of political unity, and accept the separation generously, without any foolish Machiavellian reserves, as an inevitable fact.

*   *   *

Let us now turn our attention to our policy in the West; cast a glance at our numerous family in America. It is taken as indisputably proved that the modern system of colonisation, mainly represented by England, is superior to the old colonial system of Spanish practice. To make the affirmation stronger, it is usual (I have often heard and read it) to set up a parallel, not between colony and colony, but between former colonies now emancipated from the respective mother-countries. In the case of actual colonies it is not easy to fix the degree of evolution at which each has arrived, whereas in nations which have attained to independence the results of one or other colonial system appear as clearly defined, giving character to the new nationality. And the terms of this comparison are, of course, quite evident: on the one hand the Ibero-American republics, on the other the United States of North America.

With the criteria in use to-day to judge political affairs, it is hardly necessary to say that the comparison is made to our disadvantage. The United States are a formidable nation, wealthy and apparently well-governed; they claim to exercise paternal protection over the whole American continent, and to intervene in European affairs. There have not been wanting European statesmen to belaud the perfection of their political institutions, and some have even desired to copy them. On the contrary, the republics of Hispanic origin are poor, and badly governed, they live in civil strife, with *pronunciamientos* almost a yearly occurrence.

The virtues of the Spanish race, we are told, have degenerated in America and have been changed into deadly sins. Martial valour has ended in militarism of the worst species, that form of militarism in which the soldiers want to be generals, and pride has been changed into vulgar, petulant self-infatuation. And as final proof of our incompetence, I was told by a worthy individual with whom I was discussing the matter some time since: "If in any part of Europe you mention America, they will at once understand you to mean the United States; an American is a subject of the Union, as if the Union were the whole of America.   To indicate a citizen of one of the other republics or colonies, it is not enough to say he is an American, you must add the special name of the nation to which he belongs."

Against this I advanced several arguments, somewhat in the following style. It is true that the subjects of the Union have monopolised the name of American, but this fact serves precisely to mark a difference which in time will bear its fruits, and in which I see the promise of the future superiority of the creations of our race. The difference lies in this—that we possess to the highest degree, more than any others, the power of impressing our character; a soil trodden by us soon receives the marks of our spirit, and with these the fundamental force for the constitution of a State, the territorial character. At first glance it seems a proof of superiority that a subject of the United States is recognised as such by his merely saying: "I am an American." But on closer attention we shall note that if he employs a generic title which covers also the subjects of other States, it is because he has no special name of his own, unless, indeed, he accepts the nickname of "Yankee". If, after telling us he is an American, he wants to be more specific, he cannot find a name which will differentiate him to our eyes. To say: "I am a citizen of the United States" is vague and long; to add: "I am from Illinois, Ohio, Tennessee or Kentucky" tells us nothing, and if he says he is from Carolina we shall take him for a denizen of certain Pacific isles.

On the contrary, the Republics of Spanish origin, even the most microscopic, have a special stamp which distinguishes them one from the other. When a man tells us that he is a Mexican, an Argentine, a Brazilian, a Chilean, a Peruvian, and so on, he tells us something that rounds him off, gives him a personal air; in a word, marks him with the spirit of his territory.

In this simple observation we have the key to the criticism applied to our American republics. Hence arise all the differences in their evolution and organisation, in their present and future conditions. A nation is not like an individual; it requires several centuries in order to develop. The Hispano-American nations have not yet passed out of infancy, whereas the United States started in adult age. Why this? Because the one, on receiving the influence of their territories, went back and commenced their evolution as new peoples, step by step, stumbling over all the obstacles which present themselves to new societies lacking in a clear knowledge of the course they are to take. The other has continued living an artificial life, imported from Europe, as it might live it in any other territory; in Australia, for example. The petty conflicts which in the first case disturb political life are not signs of degeneration; they are signs of excessive, ill-directed vitality, the expansiveness of young societies struggling for what men always start by struggling for: their independence and personal prestige as against the authoritarian action of organised powers. In these struggles strong bodies are produced, and from them arises true social progress, integral civilisation, which does not consist merely in the piling-up of private and public wealth, but also and mainly in the ennobling of the idea by means of art. And so the defender of the United States to whom I previously referred, and who is a great lover of music, was almost prepared to agree with me shortly afterwards that the "Habanera" by itself is worth the entire production of the United States, not excluding the sewing-machine and the telephone. The "Habanera" is a creation of the territorial spirit of the island of Cuba, which in our race engenders those profound feelings of infinite melancholy, of pleasure which melts into floods of bitterness, feelings which would not leave the slightest impress on the race to which the subjects of the United States belong.

This character which we have the power of infusing into

our political creations and by which we give arms to rebellion, strength with which afterwards to combat ourselves, is a jewel of inestimable value in the life of nationalities, but it is also a serious obstacle to the exercise of our influence. The Spaniard who settles in another country is a terrible enemy to Spain, as long as Spain keeps him to her obedience, and when he obtains his liberty he becomes a suspicious friend. He still continues to be Spanish in essence, but as his affections are fixed on another soil, his good qualities work in a direction opposed to our interests. He tolerates intellectual influence, because the bonds of subordination woven by this are subtle in extreme; but he rejects all influence manifested in material facts. Hence my opposition to all the Ibero-American Unions ever conceived or to be conceived; where our race is concerned there is no worse method of bringing about union than to publish and proclaim it with pomp and trumpet-blast. Such a procedure leads only to the setting-up of organisms which are useless, when they do not defeat their purpose.

Whenever there is talk of an Ibero-American Union I have remarked that the first thing proposed is an agreement for the protection of intellectual property—a Copyright Act—the one thing most opposed to the union that it is sought to establish. I do not believe that anyone has seriously considered setting up a "Political Confederation of Hispano-American States"; this ideal is so difficult of realisation, demands such a long time, that as things are it belongs to the realm of imagination. No other possible confederation is left, then, but an intellectual or spiritual confederation. And for this it is necessary, first, that we have ideas of our own to give unity to the work; and, secondly, that we give these ideas gratuitously, in order to facilitate their propagation. If by means of these unions we are seeking a market for our artistic productions, let us not shelter under patriotic phraseology, let us speak clearly, give things their right names and not confer a special character of patriotism on what is merely a commercial transaction.

I have never accepted as legitimate property in intellectual production; I even have my doubts about property in ideas. The fruit springs from the flower, but it is not the flower's, it is the tree's; man is, as it were, an efflorescence of the species, and his ideas belong not to him, but to the species, which nourishes and preserves them. Men are very prone to give themselves too much importance, to believe themselves each a centre of life and of the creation of ideas. It would, I believe, be juster to go back a little and seek the centre of gravity in the base, in the stage of ideological evolution into which we are born, and of which we are the humble servants. But even accepting in theory property in ideas, there is a long way to go before we reach practical ownership of the intellectual product; we must ask ourselves if such ownership is not opposed to the intimate nature of ideas and to the part these have to play in the world. Property in material things is more necessary, and still there is such a thing as forced expropriation; there has been no hesitation in carrying it out when it has seemed useful and opportune, and there are people to-day who advocate its general adoption. Socialism is no fantasy, it is a force, positive or negative, but in any case a force which is bound to influence the evolution of our legal and political institutions. Individual property is, then, subordinate to higher interests, and whenever these require it there should be no hesitation in sacrificing it; life also is a precious thing, and yet when necessary we sacrifice it for an ideal.

Intellectual property is based on a profound error. When a man's work is inspired by the idea of gain, it is well that he be stimulated by means of personal interest, but it is illogical to apply the same principle to works of science or art, which ought to have no other motive or inspiration than the love of truth or beauty. To grant patents for invention to the savant or the artist is to convert him into a scientific or artistic manufacturer, to encourage him to turn his works into articles of commerce. Thus it happens that to-day men no longer work in order to rise to great heights, to create masterpieces; the modern intellectual worker contents himself with inventing a model which will be to the taste of the public, and then multiplying this by mass production of similar and equally remunerative works; in the same way as the manufacturer who, when an article has found favour, starts to work the lode, and produce wholesale in order to satisfy the demand. Formerly we had the sorrow of seeing the genius die of hunger, now we have the pleasure of seeing many wax fat who are entirely devoid of genius.

Apart from this general reason, there is another which affects us Spaniards more closely: the weak expansive force of our intellectual production. This is no argument against the intrinsic value of our work, rather is the value heightened and increased by it. But it renders difficult the useful action of our ideas, their influence on our own country and on the countries which speak our language; countries in which we are justified in struggling to prevent the extinction of our tradition, to preserve the unity and purity of our language. Almost all the American nations, on separating from Spain, have through a spirit of rebellion been infected by what we might call the scarlatina of French ideas or, speaking more accurately, international ideas. If Spain wishes to regain her position, she must make an effort to re-establish her intellectual prestige, and then carry it to America and implant it there without any utilitarian aims. When we decided to build railways and it was found convenient to grant customs facilities to the construction materials, we did not consider the damage that our own metallurgical production would suffer. To my mind, the preservation of our idealistic supremacy over the peoples to whom we gave birth is something nobler, more transcendental, than the construction of a railroad system.

This objection, which I direct particularly against treaties concerning intellectual property, has a wider application which might be generalised in these or similar terms: the relations between Spain and the Spanish-American nations should not be ruled by the principles of international law; on the contrary, we should systematically refuse all political action which would tend to put these relations on a level with those maintained by Spain with countries of a different origin. International law, like all branches of law, is a narrow formulary which does not embrace the whole of reality. There is a public law and a private law, but there is no inter-family public law applicable to nations derived from the one stock. The mere material distinction between nations is not enough; we must take into account the character of each nationality, and set up different regulative principles, according to the degree of intimacy by which the different nations are linked. Instead of talking a lot about fraternity and treating one another like strangers, we ought to keep our mouths closed and treat one another like brothers.

The idea of universal brotherhood is Utopian, that of cordial relations between those connected by blood-ties is a very real one, and between one and the other kind there exist gradations which participate in the Utopian and the real; fraternal relations engendered by neighbourhood, fellow-citizenship, race, language, religion, history, community of interests or of culture. I have had occasion to deal with foreigners of different nations and with Spanish-Americans, and I have never been able to look upon the latter as foreigners. It is not that I have a preconceived idea or that I wish to make a display of brotherly feelings after the fashion of an orator or a propagandist, but I notice that hardly have I spoken two words to a Spanish-American than I am in intellectual communication with him. Whereas, with a foreigner, I require very extended relations, much feeling my way, before I can converse with him in entire naturalness. In the one case I am on sure ground, because I know there exists a community of ideas which makes up for lack of confidence; in the other case, I have to begin by taking my stand on the commonplaces of intercourse, until with time I gradually overcome the difficulties involved in reaching an understanding with a stranger, when one does not possess, as I do not, the flexibility necessary to sacrifice one's own ideas and feelings on the altar of social convention. I am going to relate a commonplace occurrence in which I took part by reason of my official duties, when I was living in Antwerp. It will show that an official position is no obstacle to a life based on human feeling, and also that these ideas I here express, which may seem mere words, have a very exact and practical meaning if they are accepted as a rule of conduct, and if, without being laid down in code or treaty, they come to constitute a uniform, constant criterion in the life of the great Hispanic family.

I was notified that in the Stuyvenberg Hospital a Spaniard

lay dying, and wished to speak with the representative of his country. I went there, and one of the staff led me to the ward where the dying man lay, telling me as we went that my countryman had recently arrived from the Congo, and thas there was no hope of saving his life, for he was in the last staget of a violent attack of yellow fever. I can see now that unfortunate man, more like a painted skeleton than a human being, painfully stretched on his poor bed, waging his supreme struggle with death. And I remember that his first words were of apology for giving me trouble without having any claim to do so.

"I am not a Spaniard," he said, "but they don't understand me here, and when they heard me speak Spanish, they thought it was you I wanted to speak to."

"Well, if you are not a Spaniard", I answered, "you look like one, and in any case there is no need to worry yourself."

"I am from Central America, sir, from Managua, and my parents were Portuguese; my name is Agatón Tinoco."

"Why, then," I interrupted, "you are a Spaniard three times over. I am going to sit here a while with you, and we'll smoke a cigarette like good friends, and you will tell me what you want."

"Nothing, sir, I need nothing for the little that is left me of life, I only wanted to speak to someone who understood me; for a long time I haven't had anyone to speak to. I am an unhappy man, sir, no one more unhappy in the world. If I told you about my life, you'd see I was saying the truth."

"It is enough to look at you, friend Tinoco, to be convinced that you are telling nothing but the truth. But just tell me all your troubles in full confidence, as if you had known me all your life."

And poor Agatón Tinoco related the long tale of his adventures and misfortunes, his unhappy married life, which forced him to leave his home because "though poor, he was a man of honour", his working on the Panama Canal till its conclusion, and finally his going to the Congo Free State as a settler, where he had led his hazardous existence towards the conclusion that was even then at hand, and which occurred that same night.

"Friend Tinoco," I said, after hearing his story, "you are

the greatest man I have known to this day, you have a something which belongs only to really great men, you have worked in silence and you can now leave life with the satisfaction of not having received the reward your labour deserved. If you look into yourself and compare the work of a lifetime with the reward obtained, you see that the only recompense has been a bare existence, which has ended in this hospital bed without a soul to speak to you. Whereas your work has been a noble one, you have toiled not merely for a livelihood, but have taken your share in mighty enterprises, of which others will receive the profit and the glory. And what you have done shows that the temper of your soul is strong, that you have in your veins the blood of a race of triumphant fighters, prostrate to-day and humbled through its own faults, not the least of which is the lack of fraternal spirit, the disunion which has made us the sport of the foreigner, and which has been the reason why many like you are wandering about the world, working as obscure labourers when they might be their own masters. Think of all this, and there will come a flash of pride that will lighten with its beams the last moments of your life, for it will make you see how unworthy the world is that men like you, honourable but unhappy men, should help to fertilise it with the sweat of their brows, and support it with the strength of their arms."

As I left the hospital I thought to myself: "If any 'common-sense' person had witnessed this scene they would certainly have taken me for an unbalanced, deluded being, and would have reproached me for expressing myself in such fashion to a poor, dying man, who was not likely to understand my words. I believe that Agatón Tinoco did understand me, and that he experienced a pleasure never before enjoyed in his life: that of being treated as a fellow man and judged with entire and absolute justice. The most humble minds can understand the most elevated ideas, and those who economise truth and proclaim it only when they are sure of being understood are guilty of grave error. Truth, even though not fully understood, exercises strange influences and leads by hidden ways to the most sublime ideas, such as well up spontaneously, incomprehensibly, from common souls."

Some days since I explained to my servant, a worthy but ignorant woman, the origin of the world and the mechanism of the heavens. I did not adopt the system of Copernicus, or of Tycho-Brache, or of Ptolemy, but another system which I have invented for my own entertainment, and which, for my servant, who knew nothing of these things, is as scientific as if it had been accepted by the greatest astronomers of the world. The following day I saw my servant coming in with a bunch of roses, obtained I know not how, for they are scarce in these latitudes, and handing to me without a word this unexpected, inexplicable offering. When I had the bouquet in my hand, there came into my mind the explanation I needed and I said to myself: "The ideas I planted yesterday have blossomed into these flowers."

* * *

Let us turn our eyes toward the East to see if in this direction there comes, along with the sun, the light we need so much in Spain. Spain without Portugal is mainly a Mediterranean land; would it then be strange if we found in the Mediterranean the natural centre of our political action? I believe, in fact, that if it were indispensable for us to develop our external political life, the one policy justified by our territorial position and our history would be a Mediterranean policy. Among all the supremacies that Spain might exercise in the world, none could be more flattering to us than supremacy in that sea which has been the civiliser of humanity, no motto could be more happily inscribed on our shield than the words, "*Mare Nostrum*".

But a Mediterranean policy would need to be supported by a strong naval force, and it is a question whether we can have one to-day. I am not going to chant an elegy, or to dilate on our poverty; I am willing to accept the hypothesis that a mine of pure gold has been discovered in the vicinity of Madrid, and that all we have to do is to coin it into ready cash and buy with it the most formidable collection of iron-clads that the world has ever seen. For those who look only at the outside of things, for those who believe that naval power consists in the possession of a great number of ships, the problem would then be solved; it would only remain to deck out all those vessels with the national flag and launch them in search of heroic adventures, to continue our glorious maritime tradition. To my mind, such formidable squadrons would be a danger and a hindrance. A power which does not spring spontaneous from the natural, effective strength of a nation is a cudgel in a blind man's hand. Ships are run not merely by men, but also by national ideas, and a nation lacking in the expansive force of a strongly held idea will do nothing profitable with maritime strength, ignorant of the direction in which it ought to be employed with faith and confidence. The whole of our history shows that our triumphs were due more to our spiritual energy than to our material forces, for these were always inferior to the magnitude of our undertakings. Let us not to-day attempt to change the situation and entrust our future to purely material resources. Before going outside Spain, we must forge within our territory ideas to guide our action; to push on blindly can only lead to chance, temporary victories and to certain, ultimate defeat.

Our situation does not permit us to impose our own ideas in politics, and our history is opposed to our acting the part of mere "supers". Our line of conduct, then, in the Mediterranean, as in Europe, should be that of voluntary withdrawal. But it must be admitted that in the case of the Mediterranean the situation is not so clear as when we were discussing Europe. There are numerous political questions in which Spain is deeply interested, and where withdrawal is not a plain, natural course, but can only be the result of reflection. There is not a mile of territory along the extensive Mediterranean seaboard where a political conflict is not engaged, and if we examine these one by one we shall find that they all centre round two capital, permanent matters: the Roman question and the Turkish question. In the former Spain is interested as a Catholic country, in the latter as a Christian country, and in both as a Mediterranean Power.

The first point that requires to be made clear is that which concerns the possible intervention of Spain by reason of its religious ideas; for political notions have strayed so far from their natural path that there are people who have mixed up politics with religion and confuse the interests of the country with the aspirations of individuals. When passing in summary review the policy of Philip II, I attempted to point out that there was a capital error in his policy: that of directing the action of our country along lines foreign to our interests; but that at the same time there was present an admirable purpose, that of inspiring this same action with genuinely Spanish sentiments. This point of view is a general one for all our political affairs; whatever is done, should be done honestly and sincerely, in Spanish fashion, but nothing ought to be done out of harmony with our interests. Neither religion, nor art, nor any idea however lofty, can make up in our action for the lack of national interest, for this interest embraces all those ideas, and the whole life of the territory as well, its preservation, its independence, its aggrandisement. The policy of Philip II brought us to ruin, because of his persistence, not in upholding Catholic ideas, but in maintaining, on account of those ideas, an absurd policy, contrary to Spanish interests. And the result of this sacrifice was the decadence, the division of the peninsula, the humiliation of Gibraltar and, finally, the menace of being deprived of our independence. All these disasters were links in a chain, and had their origin in the blindness with which we attempted to base our action on ideas which had no natural foundation in our real interests.

We have a palpable example of this to-day in the matter of the colonisation of Africa. Can there be anything more noble than to civilise savages, to win over new races to our religion, our laws, our language? And yet, can there be any greater absurdity than a Spanish colonial enterprise in Africa? When we are still in a state of convalescence after our American colonisation, when we possess two large colonies which, instead of affording us the strength we need, are two open, bleeding wounds, two causes of the destruction of the little we had been able to establish, how are we going to undertake new colonial enterprises? If we were to do this, we should later on receive our reward: economic disaster, civil war, a new attempt at a republic, a new attack on our independence, any of these things or others still worse.

Spain, then, ought to regard Mediterranean affairs from a purely national standpoint, and if she did intervene, it should ne without abandoning her own ideas, in her character of a Catholic nation. Let those who think these conceptions contradictory reflect for a moment, and they will convince themselves that the contradiction lies in maintaining that a nation should. ruin itself in defence of noble ideas, and thus risk, together with its own existence, the future of those same ideas.

If we consider all the questions now at issue in the Mediterranean from the point of view of our national interests, we shall without difficulty reach the conclusion that the most favourable solutions are those that involve delay. When one has not the necessary strength to force a decision, one must simply act so as to postpone a decision; and if the solution hangs fire because the opposed interests are in equilibrium, the wisest and at the same time the most convenient course is abstention. When a country is actually, positively interested in a matter, as Spain is in Morocco, abstention is fatal, because it makes plain that the country either does not recognise its vital interests, or is in such a bad way that it has to entrust them to foreign hands. But if intervention is not fully justified, abstention is the most prudent policy and reveals great political tact, because the manner in which both nations and individuals do most harm is by officiousness, the mania of interfering in what does not concern one. A man who speaks little but at the right time wins esteem, acquires authority and without seeking it is consulted in difficult matters; the restless, interfering person simply becomes a bore and a hindrance.

The Roman question bears the solution within itself; a solution logical and independent of the will of man, consequently irremediable: the annihilation of the political power established in Rome. Perhaps for the future of Catholicism and Catholic countries it might be well to deprive for ever the Pontificate of a temporal power which, when it existed, was a constant cause of rivalry between Catholic States desirous of dominating a disunited Italy, and which to-day, when no longer existent, is still a cause of discord and trouble. But even if the Sovereign Pontiff were to accept the

fait accompli and resign himself to having his independence
assured by international guarantees, this would still not end
the conflict, which is based not on persons, but on ideas, and
even more than on ideas, on reality. A theocratic city like
Rome, Jerusalem or Mecca, not to limit the question to
Catholicism, cannot be the seat of a stable political power,
for the government of a State is an operation inferior to the
governance of spiritual life, and by this fact civil authority
finds itself, in theory and in fact, under submission to
religious authority. There are only two solutions: either to
combine the two authorities in one, or to condemn political
authority to vassalage. Political authority has strength, but
it is only strength for the time being. In the long run, that
which triumphs is the idea, and what comparison can there
be between a passing political régime and an unchangeable
spiritual one?

The House of Savoy is one of those most worthy of regard
for its prestige and for the sincerity with which it has accepted
and put in practice the modern constitutional and democratic
system. After the House of Saxe-Coburg-Gotha, which in
this respect stands first, I believe there is no other in Europe
which fills to more perfection the difficult and disagreeable
part of reigning without governing. But the Savoy dynasty
is subject to many changes, to the natural ebb and flow of
temporal things, to decadence and even to extinction,
whereas the Holy See represents a spiritual dynasty,
impersonal and indestructible, which counts its rule by
centuries, which has seen the birth and death not merely of
dynasties, but of entire human societies. Between two
powers of such different spiritual strength there can be no
question of continuous struggle; the spiritual power, even if
it did not wish it, must destroy the political power; and the
blame will fall not to the former but to the latter, which has
been bold enough to engage in a contest immeasurably
beyond its strength.

The idea of political unity has no absolute value, and is
subordinate to other ideas already deep-rooted in life. In
Spain there is no Pope and we have not arrived at Iberian
unity, in Italy they might likewise accept a solution more
consonant with reality. Instead of a symmetrical nation with

Rome as capital, and the constant threat of an insoluble conflict, they might establish something less regular and perfect, but more firm and durable. The consolidation of Italian unity, as to-day existent, requires the annihilation of the Pontificate; but as this enterprise is not within the power of any dynasty, there will go on existing in the same city two antagonistic forces, one of which will triumph, the stronger—that is to say, the spiritual—without any need of outside help, against the opposition of adversaries, by the mere fact of co-existence.

The Eastern question is likewise a mixed one, political and religious, but of an entirely different order. The problem consists in destroying a domination which is out of harmony with the rest of Europe, in reducing to submission a race which is refractory to the mingling of blood and ideas. The forces brought into play are political interests and sympathies, possibly more feigned than sincere, on behalf of the Christians subjected to Turkish rule, though there are not wanting spirits inspired by genuine emotion, such as the Belgian professor, Kunth, who demand little less than the revival of the Crusades. The Mahometan power is always terrible, however low it may have fallen; like the sea it ebbs and flows; but there is no reason for its utter destruction. Nothing in the world ought to be destroyed, for everything exists for some purpose. One must broaden one's views and recognise that life is susceptible of many forms, in which there is always something good. Christianity, of its essence, is incapacitated from resorting to brutal measures; it must defend itself, but only to the point of ensuring its independence and its liberty of peaceful propagation.

For this reason, we must not confuse the protection of Christian subjects of the Turk with the purely political action of Europe in Turkey. Those who cry out against Turkish rule and call it an infamy and a disgrace to Europe start from a petty geographical concept, for, if that rule were to cease, what problem would be solved by driving the Turk into Asia Minor, where he would go on committing the same outrages which he commits to-day? We have either to expel the Turk from all territories inhabited by Christians, or we must tolerate his rule and prevent him giving rein to his fanaticism. A total expulsion is impossible, and to secure the alternative object there is no means more efficacious than to keep Turkey in Europe, where European nations can exercise combined action on a definite basis. Furthermore, Turkey in Europe is almost a spent force, which will gradually fall under the influence of Europe, whereas Turkey in Asia would not be long in lifting up its head and acquiring a terrible strength. In Europe it is removed from its territorial centre, from the nucleus of its power, and with difficulty maintains itself amid the dangers that surround it. In Asia, free from restrictions, led possibly by new men, it would be a nursery of fanatical fighters who would recommence the struggle. Recall how Islam, broken by the Crusades, renewed its attack, more furious than the first, against Europe; this time from the east, when the Turks came on the scene. Islam is dangerous if it is allowed to rule over widespread territories united in a religious federation, because Islam is not propagated among individuals, but takes the form of violent, rapid irruption in different directions, within its own geographical limits and at times spreading beyond them and attacking other peoples. Thus, a revival of Mahometanism would be possible if one of the numerous sects that are continuously springing up within it were free to extend in all directions and set up anew the unity necessary for the combat. A prudent European policy would be that of splitting up Islam, of intercepting these currents, by establishing at intermediate points centres of power which could serve as buffers between independent Mahometan States; but never the policy of completely destroying the political independence of Islam, which by the fact of its existence has a perfect right to maintain independent political powers. Any religious idea that takes root in a race, constituting a centre of authority and creating historic interests, demands to be respected in its political independence until time takes in hand its destruction and disappearance. If we wish to undermine a power, let us strive to destroy the idea on which it is based, but as long as that idea subsists, it is tyrannical to seek its oppression by force, and as well as tyrannical it is dangerous. If it were possible to reduce to vassalage all the territories now dominated by Islam, we should witness the immediate setting up of a "federation of the oppressed", and beneath the oppressive action of Europe there would begin to circulate in secret the marvellous watchword, the countersign for the day of revolt. All the petty rivalries which at present exist between Mahometan powers, rotting with inaction, would then disappear, and in their place a formidable rivalry, that between Christianity triumphant and Mahometanism defeated, humiliated, but by no means destroyed.

Neither on the north, the west or the east will Spain find any promise of aggrandisement by means of external political action. We shall discover neither a definitely marked aim for our policy, nor that superabundance of forces which impels towards unreflecting efforts, towards those instinctive enterprises which spring spontaneous from the spirit of the territory. We need to reconstitute our material forces in order to solve our internal problems, and our idealistic strength in order to exercise an influence in the sphere of our legitimate external interests, and to strengthen our prestige amongst the peoples of Hispanic stock. As regards the idealistic restoration, no one can doubt that it should be our own exclusive work. We may receive outside influences; shape a course by studying what other nations are doing and saying; but until we hispanicise our work, as long as what is external is not subjected to what is Spanish, and we keep living in our present uncertainty, we shall make no step forward. Our intellectual weakness is evidenced by the incoherence of our culture, made up of tatters of different colours, like a beggar's dress; but as regards our material restoration, opinions are not so unanimous. There are some who are still hoping for the miraculous inheritance as if we had a number of rich uncles in America. After several centuries of dragging ourselves along the ground, we are still unwilling to recognise that all our trust must be put in our own efforts, and that for the purpose of our labour, which is the important matter, we have in Spain to-day more soil, more light and more air than we need.

There are those who build hopes on the colonies, as if we did not know that with our system of colonisation the colonies cost more than they produce; that there is no hope of change in this matter and no need for it. A real colony ought to cost something to the mother-country, for to colonise is not to engage in business, but to civilise peoples and to propagate ideas. Let us leave to others the utilitarian forms of colonisation and continue ourselves with our traditional form, which, good or bad, is at any rate our own. We have advanced too far now to change our route, and even if we wished we could not take a new one, and even if we could-we should gain nothing by superimposing on a building constructed in accordance with our own ideas another story in a different style, possibly copied without understanding. We have been unable to form ideas of our own in regard to modern colonial practice; let us keep to the old ones, follow them up tenaciously, even if they are in conflict with current notions, for if we ourselves have no faith in the works of our creation, who will have it for us and what is going to be our mission in future history?

Some time ago I read a book by some English politician or traveller on *Peoples and Politics of the Far East,* in which such harsh censure was passed on our colonial action in the Philippines that I cannot quote here, from some sort of invincible repugnance, any of the judgments therein expressed. Without intending to do so, the author marks out the dividing line between the two methods of colonisation employed by the old conquistadores and the modern trader. I am not going to discuss here the relative merits of the two systems; I shall only say that I prefer the old one, as being more noble and disinterested. But this does not prevent one recognising that the modern system is useful to the countries that practise it, whereas the old system represented a loss of strength to the mother-country, which at first sight is not an advantageous result, but which in the long run bears fruit, namely, in the colonies.

We can, then, count on no help from our colonies, and it is well we should know that from them we shall only receive the same reward as from those who have already declared themselves free. We can only hope that the maintenance of our rule will not cost us too many sacrifices, and to this end we must show ourselves liberal, and renounce the "materialistic" domination to which our present intellectual prostration inclines us. More importance than to the direct administration of the colonies by the home country must be given to the maintenance of our prestige, somewhat weakened by the egoistic pretensions of those actually in the possession and enjoyment of political power.

There are some who consider that the necessary consequence of colonisation is the emancipation of the colonies. To my mind this is merely theoretical. Children likewise can emancipate themselves, and the law establishes when and how the *patria potestas* ceases. And yet many children never seek to emancipate themselves, never even think of doing so. They pass from one legal position to the other without noticing any difference, and it does not occur to them to await the day marked out by statute, so that they can say to the father: "From now on you cease in the exercise of the functions you have fulfilled up to the present." It is only in extreme cases that men are ruled by the letter of the law, and only in extreme cases that colonies struggle to win their independence. If by means of skilful policy and, better than skilful, disinterested, a just unity of ideas and feelings is maintained between the home country and the colonies, a system of autonomy can without any danger be applied, and this will lead, not to emancipation, but to a confederation of the colonies and the motherland. In this way autonomy will not be a first step toward emancipation, but the commencement of a more intimate union, obtained by the sacrifice of what I have called materialistic domination. But such delicate policies are not always practical, because they require the assistance of men specially trained for such difficult tasks, and not all countries possess men of that quality. If a régime of autonomy is set up, but the practices of the old governmental methods continued, failure is certain, and preferable to that is either frank and firmly maintained domination, or frank and loyally conceded emancipation.

This manner of judging our concerns will of course seem pessimistic, because, as I have said, we are so used to the idea that the greatness of a country is to be attained by an increase of territory or by the introduction of wealth gained in other countries or in colonies. Our notion of greatness is

still materialistic and quantitative, and anyone who attempts
to uproot and destroy such fantastic imaginings is looked
upon as a man of little faith. Suppose that in a stream of no
great volume there are two waterfalls of equal height. Two
engineers seek to utilise these for some type of manufacture;
the first sets up a small industry proportionate to the motive
power, the second builds a factory of imposing proportions
which cannot work through insufficiency of water. For those
who look at things from the outside, unfortunately the
majority, the engineer who constructs on a large scale is a
man of genius, and the one who sets up a small industry a
man of little talent, incapable of lofty ideas. For the few
who are not content with looking at the outside, but want
to know what is going on inside both buildings, the man of
genius will be thought little more than an idiot; and the one
who seemed to be of narrow views will be shown to be a man
of forethought. One, working on a large scale, has proved
his ineptitude for both great and small affairs; the other,
working on a small scale, has shown his capacity both for
small and great.

The Spanish factory has been out of working for long years
through lack of motive power. To-day it is starting afresh
because we have lightened some of the machinery, or it has
been lightened for us; and there are still people who want to
return to the old complications, instead of seeking to increase
the scanty motive power which to-day we possess. Hence the
absolute necessity of destroying our national illusions; and
such destruction is not the work of desperate spirits, but of a
noble, legitimate ambition, by means of which we are laying
the foundations of positive aggrandisement. The greatness
or the smallness of nations does not depend on the extent of
their territories or the number of their inhabitants. Under
the House of Austria, Spain was an immense nation, and by
being so fell into a state of prostration and paralysis. In the
time of Carlos II, Spain was like a dead whale floating in
the sea and proving an obstacle to shipping. On the other
hand, a few provinces separated from Spain, the United
Provinces, under the skilful rule of William of Orange, were
transformed into the political centre of Europe, and arrested
the progress of France, omnipotent at the time.

This fact, noted by Macaulay, finds a most natural explanation. The Low Countries, under Spanish domination, were mere territories inhabited by human beings; when they obtained their independence, they acquired nationality. Political union did not imply an increase of forces; on the contrary, it annulled them, for these forces were antagonistic. We wasted our energies in beating down the resistance of the Low Countries, and they wasted theirs by their struggle against our rule. Even if the union had been maintained by pacific means, there would have been no increase of strength, because the political aspirations of the two territories were opposed. Holland, once independent and inspired by its own ideals, was a nation stronger and more agile than the great Spanish Empire, which lay paralysed and powerless to co-ordinate in well-directed action its forces, since these were wasted in the attempt to hold a balance between several opposing policies.

When we are called upon to respect our traditions it must be made very clear what is understood by traditions. Spain is about to enter on a new evolution, and in it she must continue to be the Spain of tradition. This is inevitable, for we modern Spaniards descend without intermixture from the ancient Spaniards, and we are still living on the ancestral estate. The Modern Greeks have very little Hellenic blood (some think they have none at all), and yet they aspire to link up their contemporary history with the history of Ancient Greece. But what we must take from tradition is what it offers to us, imposes on us, its spirit. As far as actual events are concerned, we must examine them closely and see what real value they have, for many of them are useless and some of them harmful. The greater portion of our modern history is politically a contradiction in terms, which has brought us to the position in which we now find ourselves. If the new evolution is linked up with the preceding one and is guided by the indications given by the events of this tradition, we shall never advance a step. A nation at the height of its power may support political innovations not altogether in consonance with its territorial interests; but a nation just beginning to acquire strength afresh must be more exclusive and must not run off into dangerous adventures. Even in cases where action seems more justified, we must be able to count on ample means for carrying it through, material means, but more especially the spiritual energy, acquired by a thorough comprehension of the task undertaken, a previous knowledge of what the work is to be; in a word, "an ideal realisation of the work as the foretype of its material realisation".

One direction indicated by tradition for our external political action is that commonly designated by saying that we must carry out the last will and testament of Isabel la Católica. The future of Spain lies, we are told, in Africa, and the national aspirations are escaping through that vent, as if imprisoned in our territory and seeking freedom in flight. Here we have one more example of real pessimism; that of those who distrust the native forces of the country, and believe that it will not be great as long as some other piece of territory is not added to it, where, if no other result is obtained, we shall at least have the pleasure of seeing the national standard wave.

In this matter of African colonisation, Spain has not been able to do more than reserve to herself the dominion over that portion of the African seaboard which in the hands of foreigners might be a dangerous menace to our traditional possessions. It was not incumbent on her to undertake new colonising enterprises, especially if they were to be on the lines of the absurd and reprehensible system in vogue in Africa to-day.

There is no comparison between the African races and the American or Asiatic races. The former are at a much lower stage of evolution and cannot support a European culture. The most sensible thing would have been to scatter along the seaboard and the navigable rivers trading stations and missions, which would serve as a yeast for the fermentation of the native qualities of the Africans. But this is a work that requires much time, and to-day there is not the patience for it. Even if there were, political rivalries would soon bring it to naught. Consequently, resort has been had to direct domination, to expeditions into the interior, and, when necessary to ensure the progress of trade, to the slaughter of the races it was proposed to civilise. Such expeditions leave

Europe with ideas of redemption, they reach Africa with ideas of business; and on their return praise is not given to those who have done most to improve the lot of the black race, but to those who have killed most or amassed the greatest fortune.

Nevertheless, when reference is made in Spain to the last will of Isabel la Católica, attention is mainly fixed on the North of Africa, and to-day, necessarily, on the one point which maintains independent existence—the Moroccan Empire. This is the fourth of our cardinal points, the South, of which we had not yet treated; and there will be those who think that, having shut all the outer outlets, this one ought to remain open so that we be not entirely left in obscurity. I realise that an African policy was a very national one on the conclusion of the Reconquest, and if we had dedicated all the national forces to it we might well have established an indestructible political power, both because it was a logical development of our medieval history, and because it would not have clashed with other European interests. But time does not pass in vain, and time has brought with it great changes. The Moslem power is in such a state of prostration that it needs support in order to be preserved from speedy destruction; the resentments accumulated during the Middle Ages, though stirred up afresh from time to time, are not to-day what they were four centuries since, and finally, most important of all, we are no longer a flourishing nation, anxious for expansion, though as a matter of routine we demand expansion. We are a people who have been through the experience and received our warning, and who, owing to our defective memory, take little profit from warning and experience.

Spain has an interest, too plain to need demonstration, in keeping the territory on the other side of the Straits as far removed as possible from the political action of Europe, and this interest cannot be better served than by those who are actually serving it. If we were to allow ourselves to be influenced by those traditional motives, lacking as we do the indispensable means for completing the work of the politician and the soldier, and were to succeed in establishing our rule or protectorate in Morocco, we might possibly merely serve as forerunners to the greedy European trader. Whilst these benefited by the practical results of the change of power, we should have burdened ourselves with the hatred of the conquered race, which would see in our action the manifest cause of all the attacks directed against their racial feelings, which are exclusivist and by nature refractory to European civilisation. We should be, then, the unwilling abettors of interests contrary to our own and the contrivers of our own downfall. Our war in Africa is a clear proof that the African policy is not based on vital interests of the nation, but on popular enthusiasm, vague and indefinite. When an enterprise is undertaken at the urge of a genuine need of expansion, of opening new fields to the superabundant energies of the country, the military victory, whatever may have been the obstacles encountered, leaves more traces behind it than have been left by our latest victory.

A regeneration of the whole life of Spain can have no starting point other than the concentration of all our energies within our own territory. We must fasten with lock, chain and bolt every door by which the Spanish spirit escaped from Spain and spread itself over the four points of the compass, whence salvation is looked for even to-day. On each of those doors we must set up a sign, not of the Dantesque order to tell us "*Lasciate ogni speranza*", but another more consolatory, more deeply human, imitated from Saint Augustine: "*Nolite foras ire, in interiore Hispaniæ habitat veritas*".

§ C

IF we compare the philosophic thought of a masterpiece
of art with the thought of the nation in which it was
produced, we shall find that, independently of the
purpose of the author, the work bears a significance, which
might be called historical, in harmony with the national
history: an interpretation of the spirit of this history. And
the closer the harmony, the greater the merit of the work;
for the artist draws his strength insensibly from the mingling
of his own ideas with those of his territory, acting as a
reflector in which these ideas cross and mingle, and acquire
by their crossing and mingling a brilliance in which, when
separated, they were lacking. One of the greatest productions of our theatre is Calderón's *Life's a Dream*; in it, in a
particular psychological case which has a universal symbolic
value, the artist gives us a clear, lucid, prophetic explanation
of our own history. Spain, like Segismundo, was violently
brought out from the cavern of its obscure existence, made
up of struggles against the Africans, and thrust into the
centre of European existence, converted into lord and master
of peoples it hardly knew. When after many and extraordinary happenings, which seem more fantastic than real,
we return to consciousness in our former cave, where we
find ourselves now enchained in poverty and misery, we
ask ourselves if all that history were a reality or a dream.
The only thing that makes us doubt its being a dream is the
splendour of the glory which still gleams on us and seduces
us, like that loving image which troubled the solitude of
Segismundo and caused him to cry out: "One woman indeed
I loved—this I hold for truth—for now all else is gone—this
thing alone remains."

A people cannot, and if it could, ought not, live without

glory; but it has many ways of winning it, and moreover glory exhibits itself in various forms. There is the glory of ideas, the noblest form, which is reached by the effort of the intelligence; there is the glory of the struggle for the triumph of one country's ideas against another's; there is the glory of the fierce fight for mere material domination; there is the sadder glory of mutual annihilation in civil strife. Spain has known all these forms of glory, and for a long time past is in full enjoyment of the saddest type of all: we are living in perpetual civil war. Our temperament, excited but weakened by endless periods of strife, is incapable of transforming itself, of finding a pacific means of expression, of speaking by more human signs than those of arms. So we see that those who become enamoured of an idea convert it into a weapon of combat. They do not really fight in order that the idea may triumph; they fight because the idea requires an outward form in which to take shape; and instead of positive, creative forms, they accept the negative, destructive ones: argument, not as a work of art, but as an instrument of destruction; tumult, mutiny, revolution, war. In this way ideas, in place of serving to create durable effects, which by setting up something new will indirectly break down the old and useless, serve for the destruction, devastation, annihilation of everything and themselves perish amid the ruins.

Our country must be brought to find scope for its energies and feelings in rational ways, and to this end new spiritual life must be infused into the individual, the city and the State. We have seen that our political organisation is independent of external affairs; there is no outside cause which urges us to adopt this or that form of government. Our aspirations towards what lies outside our shore are either baseless or Utopian, realisable at such a far-off period that it is impossible for their sake to distract our attention and to continue living on expectations. The only useful conclusion to be drawn from a study of possible external interests is that we ought to strengthen the organisation we actually possess, and acquire more intensive intellectual strength, because our historic role requires us to change our action from material to spiritual. Spain was the first European nation to grow great by a policy of expansion and conquest, she

was the first to decay and to bring to an end the material
stage of her evolution; she must now be the first to work
towards a social and political regeneration of an entirely
new order. Consequently, her position is different from that
of other European nations. She ought to imitate none of
these, but herself initiate a new procedure, in harmony with
facts which are also new in history. Neither French, nor
German, nor English ideas, nor any other that may afterwards be in vogue, can be of service to us, because we,
though inferior in political influence, are superior, more
advanced, in respect of the stage our natural evolution has
reached. By the fact of having lost our power of domination
(and every country will come eventually to lose it), our
nation has entered on a new phase of its historic life, and
must find out what course is indicated by its present interests
and by its tradition.

The political problem that has to be solved by Spain has
no clearly marked precedent in history. A founder-nation
of numerous other nations, after a long period of decadence,
attempts to reconstitute itself as a political force animated
by new sentiments of expansion. What form should this
second evolution take in order to link up with the former
without breaking the historic unity to which one and the
other ought to be subordinate? For we are taking unity to
be a fact, not an artifice; it would be a mere artifice to break
with tradition, and to attempt to commence living a new life,
as if we were a new people, fresh baked from the oven. Spain
may have courses marked out for it different from those
indicated by her previous history, but a clear break with the
past would be a violation of natural laws, a cowardly
desertion of our duty, a sacrifice of the real for the imaginary.
No new external policy can lead us to the restoration of the
material greatness of Spain, to the winning back of the high
rank it once held; such new enterprises would be like the
pretensions of unrepentant old fools who, instead of dedicat-
ing themselves with resignation to the memory of their noble,
youthful loves, drag themselves along in search of new and
feigned amours, of purchased caresses, of parodies, ridiculous
when not repugnant, of the fairer scenes of their emotional
life.

On the other hand, if by the sole effort of our intelligence we could succeed in reconstituting the union of all the Hispanic peoples, and inspiring into them the cult of the same ideals, of our ideals, we should then fulfil a great historic mission and give birth to a great, new creation, something original in the annals of history. And in fulfilling that mission we should be working for the benefit not of a generous ideal without practical utility, but of our own interests, interests more important than the conquest of a few strips of territory. Since we have exhausted our forces of material expansion, we must now change our tactics, and bring into action forces which are never exhausted, those of the mind. These are now lying latent in Spain, but can, when developed, carry us on to great creations which, by satisfying our aspiration towards a noble and glorious existence, may serve as the political instrument required for the task we have to realise. From this point of view, the political questions to which Spain preferentially gives her attention are worthy simply of contempt. We are living as imitators, when we ought to be creators; we are trying to direct our affairs by the example of those who have come after us; we are busy searching for forms of government, for external policies, without ever considering what we are going to put into them to prevent them being empty vessels.

The organisation of the public powers is no very difficult matter; it requires no extraordinary knowledge or art, merely broadmindedness and good will. A society which understands its own interests will organise power as rapidly as possible, and pass on to other more important matters. A nation that lives a whole century in process of constitution cannot be taken seriously; by that mere fact it makes evident that it does not know where it is going, and through not knowing this passes the time in discussion as to where it ought to go. Public power is mere scaffolding; it ought to be solidly fixed, so that work can go on over it without fear of accident; the essential thing being that, in cne fashion or other, the work be done. The work of the restoration of Spain is still at the foundations; the scaffolding rises to where in time the roof will be, and there are still restless, senseless people who are not yet satisfied. The lack of fixedness observable in the direction of our general policy is merely a reflection of the lack of ideas in the country, of the universal tendency to solve every problem by external assistance, not by native effort. The country looks to some external action, indefinite and uncomprehended, to raise up our lost prestige; the towns live in beggary, both of ideas and material resources, and look to the State for everything. Their functions are purely administrative and material; when they conceive anything on a large scale, it is not qualitative but quantitative, an extension of the town limits, that is, merely a small-scale reduction of the notion of national aggrandisement by means of annexation of territory that we do not need. Individuals work just enough to solve the problem of not working at all, of substituting for personal labour requiring energy and effort some routine employment, whether suited or not to the scanty knowledge and skill they have acquired. In a word, hopes are always centred in some favourable external change, never in constant and intelligent labour.

Given these notions, political changes only serve to make worse our already vitiated instincts. We have a very plain example of this in our universities. It was thought to find a remedy for our intellectual penury by infusing new life into our teaching centres, by transforming them from enclosed precincts into fields open, as it was said, to the diffusion of all kinds of knowledge. The idea was a good one, if it had not been limited to a mere change of label. The freedom of the professorial chair is neither good nor bad in itself; it is a system which, like the old one, may be of profit or not, according as it is well- or ill-used. The exclusive type of education would be good if the principles which inspired it were sufficiently vigorous, without need of the stirrings of controversy, to maintain in fruitful life the sciences and arts of the nation. This system would give us a culture somewhat narrow in outlook and incomplete, but in exchange we would have unity of thought and action. It is only when doctrines decay and lose their creative force that it becomes necessary to introduce fresh leaven to cause them to ferment anew. Freedom of teaching (I am not speaking of the ridiculous forms it has in practice taken in Spain) has also, like everything else, two aspects; its weak side is the lack of congruity between the different doctrines, the intellectual disequilibrium which contradictory ideas generally produce in weak heads; its good side is the impulse it gives to the mind to choose in absolute independence a course for itself and to rise to original conceptions. We have chosen the evil, not the good. We were told that Catholic education was condemning us to mental atrophy; "free" education is rapidly leading us to brutishness. We become aware that in this or the other university there are pseudo-scientific rivalries, because we read or hear that the supporters of the opposing bands have stirred up a tumult or come to blows like roughs. What we had not before nor have now, with some honourable exceptions, are men who cultivate science scientifically and art artistically; all systems of weights and measures have been lost, save one alone, that of official posts. Whatever be the kind and merit of a work, we know that it will only win esteem when its author occupies a good position in the social scale. Hence the subordination of all our output, our very scanty output, to purely external interests; and we must even give credit to those who so subordinate their work, for the generality simply abandon it altogether and content themselves with their place in the official ranks. The universities, like the State and the municipalities, are empty organisms; they are not bad in themselves, or in need of change; we need not smash the machine, what we have to do is to feed ideas into it so that it will not stand useless. If anything is to be smashed, let us smash the universal artifice by which we live, hoping for everything from outside and giving merely external form to our activities. We shall then change charlatanism into healthy, useful thought, and the external conflict which destroys into the internal conflict which creates. That is the way to work in order to fortify the public powers, that is the way to reform our institutions.

*   *   *

If I were brought into consultation as a spiritual physician, to make a diagnosis of the malady from which we Spaniards are suffering (for there is a malady, and one very difficult to cure), I should say that the disease is to be designated as "lack of will-power", or in more scientific language by the Greek word *"aboulia"*, which means the same thing: extinction or grave weakening of the will. I should support this opinion, were it necessary, by texts from authorities and detailed reports of clinical cases, for from Esquirol and Maudsley to Ribot and Janet there is a long series of doctors and psychologists who have studied this infirmity, in which, perhaps more than in any other, there is clearly revealed the influence of mental disorders on organic functions.

There is a common form of *aboulia* which we all know and at times suffer from. Who has not been at some time overtaken by that perplexity of mind, due to weakened strength or the lethargy following on a period of inaction, in which the will, lacking some dominant idea to impel it, hesitating between opposed motives which sway it, or dominated by an abstract, unrealisable idea, remains irresolute, not knowing what to do and not deciding to do anything? When such a situation from being temporary becomes chronic, we have the case of *aboulia*, shown outwardly by the repugnance of the will to perform free acts. In the sufferer from *aboulia* there is an initiation of effort, which shows that the will has not been completely destroyed; but the movement is a very weak one and rarely reaches its term. This is not a disordered movement to be confused with those produced by ataxia; in the one case there is weakness, in the other lack of co-ordination. So much is this so, that in cases of *aboulia*, apart from free acts, the rest, the purely instinctive, or those produced by suggestion are carried out in orderly fashion.

The intellectual symptoms of *aboulia* are many: the attention is weakened in proportion to the newness or strangeness of the object on which it is required to be fixed; the understanding seems to be petrified, incapable of assimilating new ideas; it. is only active in recalling the memory of past happenings; but if it does succeed in acquiring a new idea, through lack of any counterbalance it changes from atony into exaltation, into the "fixed idea" which leads to "violent impulse".

There are in all diseases, alongside the typical cases,

others of allied nature. In the present instance, the number of the first kind is not very great, that of the second overwhelming. In Spain, for example, there are numerous cases of weak will, with the result that we have a state of "collective *aboulia*". I am no upholder of that metaphorical sociology which looks upon nations as organisms equally determined as are individuals. Society is only a resultant of the forces of individuals: in proportion as these are organised, they can perform actions which are weak or strong, or which cancel out by opposition, and the total product will always share in the character of those who take part in its creation. The individual, in his turn, is a small-scale reproduction of society; his physiological existence is made up of a combination of internal vital energy with external forces absorbed and assimilated. Spiritual life develops in analogous fashion, the mind being nourished by the ideal elements which society preserves, as it were, in store, to use the words of Fouillée. In this sense, I believe we can profitably apply individual psychology to social states, and the pathology of mind to the pathology of politics.

In our country we find manifested all the symptoms of the disease from which the majority of Spaniards suffer. Physiological and instinctive acts are performed; just as the individual organism functions in order to live, society also has to function for its existence. Work which is free for the individual is for society necessary, unless we are dealing with nomad peoples. Similarly, the concealing of income from the investigations of the Treasury is a social act as instinctive as shutting one's eyes when threatened with a blow. But the acts we do not find performed are those of free purpose, such as a conscious intervention in the direction of public business. If in practical life *aboulia* makes its presence known by lack of action, in the intellectual sphere it is characterised by lack of attention. For some time past our country has been, so to speak, wandering aimlessly about in the world. Generally, nothing interests it, nothing urges it; but all of a sudden an idea becomes fixed, and, finding no others to counterbalance it, results in headlong impulse. In these latter years we have had several typically impulsive movements produced by fixed ideas: the integrity of the fatherland, historical justice, and the like. All our intellectual products suffer from this lack of equilibrium, from this optical illusion; we have no simultaneous vision of things as they are each in its proper place; we see them in patches, some to-day, others to-morrow. What one day is well in the foreground, hiding all the rest, is forgotten the next day, because some other has come forward in its place.

Many theories have been put forward to explain the genesis of *aboulia*. It was at one time looked upon as a form of madness, and alienists gave it the name of "contact mania", attending only to the external manifestation characteristic of the malady. According to this theory, our nation might be looked upon as a cage of extraordinary beings attacked by a strange mania, that of not being able to put up with one another. I do not accept this theory, because, as I have said, in sufferers from *aboulia* the disturbances of the will do not indicate lack of co-ordination, but weakening of functional energy. With the exception of Ribot, who is inclined to believe that the cause of this curious pathological state is of a sentimental order, due to lack of desire, all pathologists, working on different lines, have now reached the conclusion that the cause is a disturbance of the intellectual functions. Janet, who published, some years ago, an interesting study from personal observation on a case of "*aboulia* with fixed ideas", believes that the weakening of will-power comes from lack of attention, and, consequently, of perception. Although these symptoms appear constantly, I am of opinion that it is not possible to establish a relation of cause and effect. Intellectual faculties, when exteriorised, participate in will-movement, and it can be equally well affirmed that the will is weakened because attention is fluctuating and perception confused, as that attention is not active nor perception clear because the will is not intense.

A spiritual activity exteriorised is a reflection of an interior activity; this is axiomatic as regards the act of creation, for how can one conceive an empty brain behind the work of savant or artist, or a cold spirit beneath the transports of passion? Just as the lack of material appetite indicates a lessening of digesti·e activity, so a lack of spiritual appetite, manifested in the slackness of those faculties which result in external acts, reveals a weakening of that internal assimilating energy which the Aristotelians called "active intelligence", the Positivist named "synthetic sense", and which is nothing else than the intelligence itself functioning in accordance with the law of association.   To my mind, then, the cause of *aboulia* is the weakening of this synthetic sense, this faculty of associating representations.   In relation to the past, the intelligence functions regularly, because memory undertakes to reproduce ideas whose association has been already formed.   But with regard to the present, the mental labour which for healthy individuals is easy and agreeable, just as digestion is for those with a good appetite, becomes difficult and painful for those suffering from lack of will-power.   The representations offered by the senses are changed· into intellectual data, some of which, the majority, disappear without leaving a trace; others become painfully fixed, like nails driven into the brain, and produce the gravest disorders.

What relation is there between the weakening of the synthetic sense and the lack of will-power?   The same as between idea and free-act, such a close one that both have come to be included under one entity; hence the "idea-force", the "idea-will", and other terms of the philosophy in fashion.   In the voluntary act there are two elements which engender a third: an individual and an idea which produce an energy.   The individual bears within himself, unified in his personality, the elements received through heredity, acquired by toil and by the simple fact of living in society. The representation or idea is in the individual like the lines and colours in a picture; on the one canvas one can trace numberless lines and combine numberless colours. According as the law of association prevails or not, from this variety will arise either an artistic creation or a confused, formless daub.   When the representations of the mind are grouped around central ideas they become clearer the more they increase in number.   Immense, then, is the value of this faculty of synthesis; without it intellectual efforts are vain and even defeat their purpose, like the brush-strokes of a blind man trying to paint a picture.   In the victim of *aboulia* ideas lack their necessary condition: associability.   Consequently, his intellectual efforts are devoid of efficacy; in some cases the fixed idea, that which most forcibly influences the will, leads to violent, impulsive decision, which has been confused with that of the madman; in other cases the abstract idea or the idea reproduced by memory engenders a weak, impotent, unrealisable desire. There are none of those fruitful, healthy desires which spring from reflective study and attentive observation of reality.

The collective will functions in an analogous manner. Societies possess personality, ideas, energies. Though the collective conscience does not manifest itself in such a clear and determined way as that of an individual, it exists and functions through acts which are collective, though they appear to be concentrated in a limited number of minds. If the idea of a great statesman was arbitrary or capricious, foreign to the general thought and feeling, it could not advance a step. What appears to be the original idea of one man is only the interpretation of the ideas or vague indeterminate desires which society experiences, without being able to give them fitting and exact expression. And as long as a nation's thought is not clearly defined, its action must be weak, indecisive, transitory. The synthetic sense in society, and in particular in its directors, is the capacity to work consciously, to realise aright its destinies. There are nations in which one can observe, beyond all the secondary divergencies, a rare and constant unanimity in understanding their own interests. This understanding seems as clear as that of an individual who, at a given moment, recalling his past and examining his present situation, realises precisely what he is and what he stands for.

In other societies, on the contrary, disaccord prevails; there come into play those partial interests which correspond to isolated ideas in the individual. These are not synthetised in a common interest, because there is lacking the working intelligence, the interior energy which would fuse them. These separate representations are irreducible, and the activity derived from them is bound to be weak and inconstant. Sometimes the motive will be tradition, which, whatever one may think of it, can never produce an energetic impulse, because in the life of the intellect the past, though a strong centre of resistance, is a feeble principle of action. At other times the impulse will be due to some outside force; for feeble societies, like inferior artists, supply by imitation the defects of their own inspiration. Now some secondary interest will push itself forward, and produce deviation, retrogression, confusion in the march of society; again the idea of the general interest, guessed at rather than perceived, will create a momentary state of false energy and deceptive activity; always there will be lacking the clear, precise idea of the common interest, and the calm, constant action which tends to realise it.

From all this can be inferred how foolish it is to expect that our country will regain its lost strength by means of external activities. If in the little that we do to-day our weakness is revealed, what would happen if we attempted to accelerate the movement? The restoration of our strength demands a prudent policy of slow and gradual advance, of absolute subordination of action to intelligence. In order that this action may be useful and productive, we must think before we act, and in order to think the first thing necessary is to have a head. For a long time past this important organ has been missing in us, and we must create it at whatever cost. I am not one of those who call for a genius invested with dictatorship; a genius would be an artificial head which would leave us in a worse state than the present. The origin of our decadence and of our actual prostration is to be found in our excess of action, in our having undertaken enterprises out of all proportion to our powers. A new dictatorial genius would utilise us as blind forces, and on his disappearance, the guiding force disappearing with him, we would sink back once again, without having made a step forward in the work of re-establishing our power, which should reside in all the individuals of the country, and be based on the common individual effort.

*   *   *

It will have been noted that the central motive of my ideas is the restoration of the spiritual life of Spain; but it is necessary to clarify this concept, for Spanish words have been so damaged by ill-use that they have no meaning unless commented on and explained. When I speak of spiritual restoration, it is not in order to round off a period by using fine-sounding phrases; I speak with all the simplicity of a schoolmaster. I am not going to propose the setting up of new teaching centres, or a new education code; all legislation is inefficacious as long as evil practices are not destroyed, and to destroy these the law is much less useful than individual efforts. As regards teaching centres, such as they are to-day, if half of them were suppressed it would be no great loss. I have been in close relations with more than two thousand fellow students, and, with the exception of three or four, none of them studied more than was necessary to fill, or rather to obtain, a remunerative post. Our teaching centres are soulless buildings; at most they furnish knowledge, they do not inspire a love of knowledge for its own sake, the initial impulse which will render study fruitful when the student is free from supervision. If, in this con- nection, any attempt were to be made by the authorities, the most advantageous change would be to substitute for the examinations now in vogue a presentation of "work done" by the candidates. Instead of those exhibitions of charlatanism, where, as in a horse race, victory goes not to the most intelligent, but to the longest-winded and the longest-legged, I would introduce a kind of intimate reunion, where examiners and examinees would be brought into direct contact, discussion would be straightforward, the personal work presented by each candidate would be judged, and an estimate made of each one's capacity, or rather of his possible utility to the country. Under such a system, youths who now waste their time preparing to enter on this or that fixed step in the professional ladder, learning to answer by heart stupid, incoherent questions, would be obliged to produce work from among which it would not be strange that some might prove to be meritorious.

The main burden of the struggle should, to my mind, be borne by intelligent and disinterested persons who realise the need of re-establishing our prestige; we have few examples of men possessed of silent patriotism, but when one appears he alone is worth a university. But in order that

I—s

individual efforts may exert beneficent influence on the
nation, they must be directed by a firm hand, for in Spain
it is not enough to launch ideas, they must first be rendered
harmless.

By reason of the state of intellectual prostration in which
we lie, there is an irresistible tendency to transform ideas into
instruments of warfare. The most usual thing is to pay no
attention to what is said or written, but if by chance any
attention is paid, the idea becomes a fixed one and is
translated into wild impulse. Hence those who propagate
systematic ideas, which give rise to new and violent factions,
instead of doing good, do harm, because they keep men's
minds at an unhealthy tension. Ideas such as these, which
incite to strife, I call "jagged" ideas, and contrariwise, such
as inspire love of peace I call "round". This book which
I am writing contains only "round" ideas. I am not sure
whether it will be read, and I suspect if anyone reads he will
pay no heed, but I am convinced that if anyone were to heed
me there would be one fighter less and one worker more.

The process that I make use of to "round off" my ideas is
within the reach of everyone. We often find that in a
family opinions differ: for example (the case is frequent),
the children take up different professions, go their different
ways, or find themselves in opposition over money matters,
and brotherly feelings are put to the proof. In some families
the idea of unity is stronger than the partial interests;
nobody yields completely, but they all give in sufficiently to
prevent a breakaway. In others unity is destroyed by vanity,
pride or selfishness, and a struggle supervenes, much more
bitter than among strangers; for among strangers the
struggle is for the defence of opposed ideas or interests,
whereas in the case of a family there is the additional
struggle to burst the ties of kinship. And how can ideas and
interests be advanced by this blind and inveterate struggle?
People think that in order to bear witness to their faith in an
idea they must fight to assure its triumph, and this absurd
belief is held by all those in Spain who convert ideas into
weapons of destruction. The great believers have been
martyrs; they have fallen resisting, not attacking. Those who
resort to force to defend their ideas make it clear, by this

fact alone, that they have neither faith nor conviction, that
they are merely commonplace, ambitious men who desire
immediate victory in order to adorn their brows with
spurious laurels and to receive prompt payment for their
labours.

Ideas gain nothing by declaring war on other ideas; they
are much more noble when they subdue themselves to
living in society, and it is to bring this about that we must
set to work in Spain. It should be lawful to profess, propagate
and defend all kinds of ideas, but "intellectually", not after
the fashion of savages. From the moment that an idea
accepts the fact of the intellectual solidarity of a nation and
adapts itself so as not to offend fraternal sentiments, it is
transformed into a most useful force, because it incites men
to individual effort. Instead of creating exclusive, destructive
factions, it creates sound and healthy minds, which produce
not words, but, something more important, deeds.

Almost all the outstanding men who for the last twenty
years have been engaged in throwing down the little that
remained of our nation, have now confessed their error and
given up the second part of their lives to remaking what they
had unmade in the first. This conduct, worthy of all praise,
ought to teach a lesson to the new generation who are
beginning to push their way in the world, and to the beardless
youths in our colleges and universities. We have plenty of
those over-clever people who imitate only too well the first
part of this conduct and are now starting on the work of
demolition, leaving repentance for later years, when, having
satisfied the craving of personal ambition, they may with
more patience bear the grief of seeing their country still in
ruins. It would be more rational to imitate the latter part
of the conduct, and not deliberately to seek an opportunity
of having to repent later on.

Apart from that essential quality of ideas, it seems to me
that it would be of great advantage, in order to render them
more useful and fitted to the work of our spiritual restoration,
if they were set out in simple form, freed from the useless
trappings with which they are to-day enshrouded by the
dictates of fashion. It would be an excellent thing if all those
who take a pen in their hands were to imagine that as yet

there had not been invented either printing, or cheap paper, or copyright law. The general opinion to-day favours the ponderous tome, perhaps because it is easier to make up one's mind not to read it. A big book, it is thought, gives importance to its author, even if it is bad; it inspires respect and takes up a lot of room on library shelves. There is no possible excuse for a small book: if good, it will be looked upon as a mere essay, a promise of something greater; if bad, it will only serve to bring the author into ridicule. My idea is exactly the opposite. A big book, it seems to me, good or bad, soon becomes so much dead weight on the library shelves. A small book, if bad, shows its uselessness at glance, and dies straightway: if good, it may serve as a manual or breviary, of general use by reason of its portability and cheapness, and its efficacy for the propagation of the ideas it contains. That I hold to this opinion is shown in practical proof by this very work. On its first conception it called for two volumes of more than average size, but it ended by submitting to my will and has contented itself with some couple of hundred pages. The man with a firm will can say in that number of pages all he has to say, and even many things he ought not to say.

I have faith in the spiritual future of Spain—in this matter I am possibly too much of an optimist. A new material aggrandisement would never obscure our past greatness; a new intellectual burgeoning would make of our Golden Age a mere forerunner of the Golden Age which I am confident is to come. For in our labours we shall have on our side a force unrealised to-day, latent in the life of our nation; just as in the simile with which I started this book there were latent in the soul of the woman, married against her will and a mother contrary to her desire, the noblest and purest sentiments of virginity. This mysterious force lies within us, though it has not yet manifested itself; it accompanies and watches over us; to-day it results in weak, disorganised action, to-morrow it will be heat and light, even, if need be, electricity and magnetism.

Here is a fact worthy of our close attention. How are we to explain that, the settlers in Europe being generally of a common stock, it is the Greeks who have been, and still are,

the spiritual dictators of all the other Aryan or Indo-
European groups? The reason is clear: whereas the other
groups remained isolated in their new territories, Greece
kept in contact with Asia and received the germs of its
culture from the Semitic races. The Indo-Europeans have
admirable qualities, but they lack one most essential for life:
the fire of ideas which engenders original creations; they are
valiant, active, tenacious organisers and conquerors, but
they are not spontaneous creators. An eminent German
professor, Ihering, author of a profound work on the pre-
history of the Indo-Europeans, has made a careful study of
the influence of Aryan immigration on the ancient organisation of Rome, from which he concludes that this organisation
dates from the period of the immigrations. Those tribal
bands, set in motion and advancing through unknown
territories, were obliged to create an authority competent to
regulate their progress. When they settled down definitely,
these now useless authorities were transformed into institutions or "survivals", in which afterwards it has been thought
to find a purely ideal religious conception. Thus, for
example, the *ver sacrum* was a reminiscence of the spring
season, in which the march, suspended during the winter,
was resumed. The *pontifices* were in their origin builders of
bridges, and their influence arose from the special importance
which, in actual fact, the migrants must have attached to
bridge-building over the rivers which hindered their passage.
The Roman augurs were not prophets filled with divine
inspiration; they were in origin scouts, who, by tracks on the
ground, the songs of birds, by astronomical and other
signs—the "auspices"—decided the most suitable or the
safest route. If it were possible to know thoroughly the
origins of the primitive institutions of the Aryan peoples, we
might find that they were all inspired by dire necessity, not
by spontaneous impulse. When Greco-Roman culture had
lost its force, and something new was required, there came
on the scene Christianity, a Semitic creation, so that the
two pillars which support the social edifice inhabited by
us—Hellenism and Christianity—are two spiritual forces
which, by very different roads, have reached us from the
Semitic peoples. In general, it may be laid down as a law of

history that wherever the Indo-European race comes in contact with the Semitic, there follows a new and vigorous Renaissance. Spain, invaded and dominated by the Barbarians, takes a backward step towards a false, artificial organisation; when the Moors come, it more than recovers lost ground and acquires the most energetic form of individualism, that of the feelings, which reaches its purest form of expression in our mystics. The Moors did not endow us with ideas, their influence was not intellectual, but psychological. The distance that lies between a primitive Christian martyr and Saint Teresa marks the road traversed by the Spanish spirit in eight centuries of struggle against the Moors. Those, then, who with systematic scorn and contempt deny any Moorish influence on our spiritual evolution are guilty of a psychological crime and render themselves incapable of understanding the Spanish character.

Our Renaissance was not a classical, it was a national one. Though it produced some masterpieces, it remained incomplete, as I have said, on account of the historical sidetracks into which fate led us. But as the impelling force lies in the ethnical or psychical constitution which the different crossings of races has given to the Spanish type, as it exists to-day, we must have confidence in the future. That force which to-day is a hindrance to the ordered life of the nation, because it is applied where it should not be applied, must be turned back on itself; the indisciplined individualism which to-day weakens us and prevents us from lifting our heads must become one day an interior, creative individualism, which will lead us to our great triumph in the realm of ideas.

All nations possess a type, real or imaginary, in which they incarnate their own special qualities. In all literatures we find a masterpiece, in which the type-man is represented as in action, as coming into contact with the society of his time, and as undergoing a long series of trials in which the temper of his spirit, which is the spirit of his race, is assayed. Ulysses is the Greek *par excellence*, in him are united all the virtues of the Aryan—prudence, constancy, effort, self-control, with Semitic astuteness and fertility of resource. Compare him with any of the leaders of Germanic peoples, and we shall see, with the utmost precision, the proportion of the Greek spirit that is due to Semitic influence. Our Ulysses is Don Quixote, and in Don Quixote we are immediately aware of a spiritual metamorphosis. The type has undergone purification, and in order to act must free itself from the burden of material preoccupations, loading them on to a squire, Sancho Panza. In this way he proceeds in complete ease, and his action is an endless creation, a human prodigy, in which every conception is idealised. Don Quixote did not exist in Spain before the Moors came, nor during their stay, but after the conclusion of the Reconquest. Without the Moors, Don Quixote and Sancho Panza would have been a single individual, an imitation of Ulysses. If we look outside Spain for a modern Ulysses, we shall find none to surpass the Anglo-Saxon Ulysses, Robinson Crusoe. The Italian Ulysses is a theologian, Dante himself in his *Divina Commedia*; the German Ulysses a philosopher, Doctor Faustus; and neither of the two is a Ulysses of flesh and blood. Robinson is a natural Ulysses, but on a very reduced scale; his Semitism is opaque, his light a borrowed one. He is ingenious only in his struggles with nature, he is capable of reconstructing a material civilisation, he is a man who aspires to command, to the "exterior" government of other men, but his soul lacks expression and cannot enter into communion with other souls. Sancho Panza, after learning how to read and write, might be a Robinson Crusoe, and Robinson Crusoe, finding himself in a difficulty, might tone down his air of superiority and submit to be Don Quixote's squire.

Just as I believe that for enterprises of material conquest many European countries are superior to us, so do I believe that for the creation of ideas there is none with finer natural aptitude than ourselves. Our spirit seems rude, because it has been coarsened by brutal strife; it seems flabby, because it has been nourished on ridiculous notions, copied without discernment from outside; and it seems unoriginal, because it has lost the bold faith in its own ideas, and looks outside for what it has within. We must make a collective act of contrition, we must return to our natural form, though this dangerous operation leave many in sorry plight. In this way, we shall have spiritual food for ourselves and for our family, now wandering about the world begging for it; and our material conquests may yet be fruitful, because after our rebirth we shall have myriads of our own race on whom to impress the seal of our spirit.

NOTES

Page 25. The translator has had to take liberties with the first paragraph. Ganivet was well aware of the theological distinction between the Virgin Birth and the Immaculate Conception. It was the latter dogma, not formally defined till the nineteenth century, that was so strenuously defended in Spain. The analogy he wishes to draw is with the Virgin Birth, but he persisted, in spite of the protests of Unamuno and other friends, in speaking here of the Immaculate Conception. He had a theory about the matter which satisfied no one but himself.

Page 38. J. L. Balmes (1810-1848), Catalan priest, philosophical and political writer.

Page 46. " House with two doors . . . "; Spanish proverb, used by Calderón as title of one of his plays.

Page 48. E. Castelar (1832-1899), Republican leader famed for his oratory.

Page 56. St. Crispin is in Spain the patron of bootmakers.

Page 66. La Beltraneja, so-called by popular attribution of her paternity to Beltran, the queen's favourite.

Page 66. Partidas—the Code formulated by Alfonso X, the Wise (reigned 1252-1284).

Page .67. *Los Amantes de Teruel*. The legend was treated dramatically by Rey de Artieda in 1581 and by Hartzenbusch in 1837.

Page 71. Moratín's *Comedia Nueva* (1792) ridiculed the playwrights of his day.

Page 80. Comuneros, name given to the party who rose in revolt against innovations introduced into Spain by Charles V.

Page 84. Habanera, music and dance characteristic of Cuba.

The patience of the reader will be specially needed in the last section, where Ganivet is so fascinated with his theory of *aboulia* as applied to the Spanish mind that he enlarges on its psychological aspects as studied in contemporary medical literature.